The Raid On St. Nazaire

Andy Ryan

This book is the third of the 'They Who Dared' Series.

The other books in the series are:

BRAVO TEN

THE RHODESIAN SAS: Their Most Daring Missions

All books by Andy Ryan are available from Amazon
In both eBook & paperback formats.

The copyright to this book is owned by the author. All rights reserved. No part of this publication may be reproduced, stored in a retrieval system, or transmitted in any form, electronic, photocopying, mechanical, recording or otherwise, without prior permission from the author.

This Book uses UK spelling

List of Illustrations

Illustrations by Andy Ryan

HMS Campbeltown before and After conversion

The outward journey

The Loire estuary, defences & the Flotilla approach route

St. Nazaire & the Intended targets

HMS Campbeltown

Before Conversion

After Conversion

The Outward Journey

The Loire Estuary, Defences & Approach Route

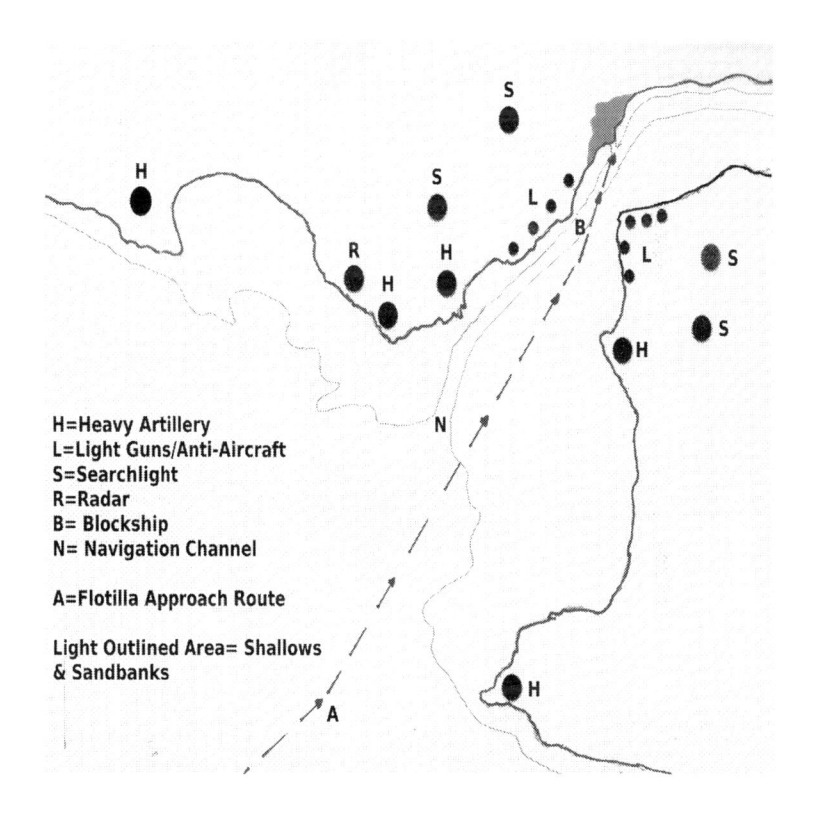

H=Heavy Artillery
L=Light Guns/Anti-Aircraft
S=Searchlight
R=Radar
B= Blockship
N= Navigation Channel

A=Flotilla Approach Route

Light Outlined Area= Shallows & Sandbanks

St. Nazaire Port

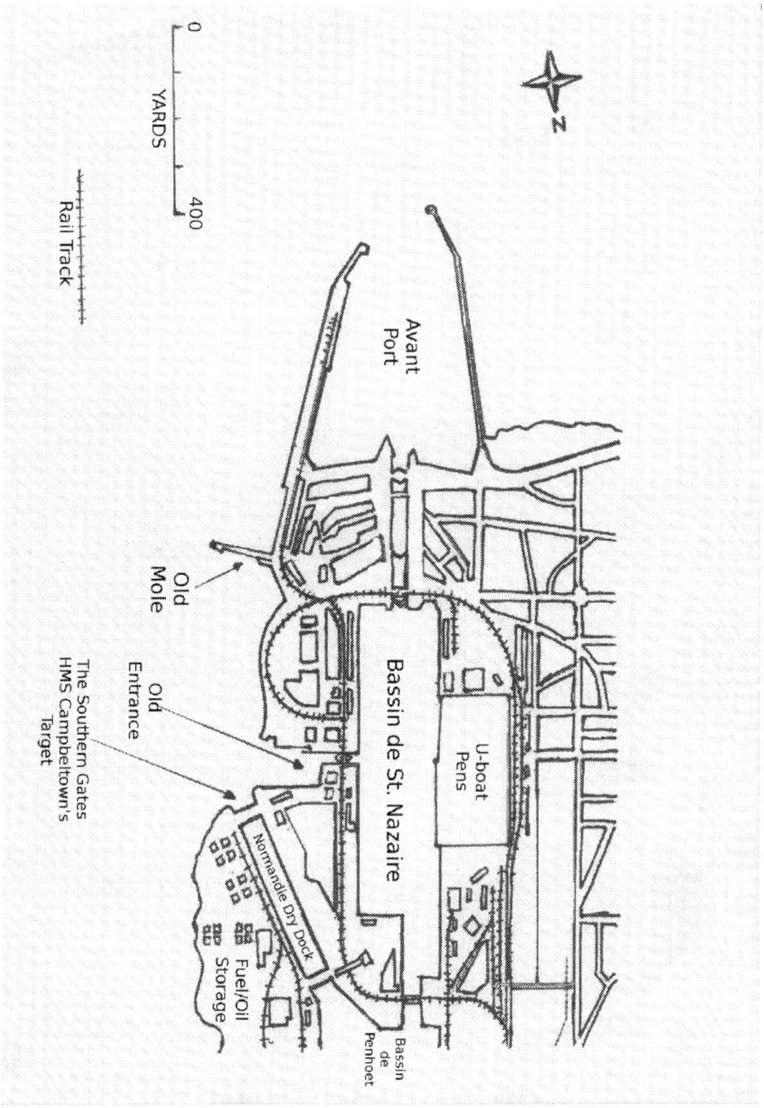
N
0
YARDS
400
Rail Track
Avant Port
Old Mole
Bassin de St. Nazaire
U-boat Pens
Old Entrance
The Southern Gates HMS Campbeltown's Target
Normandie Dry Dock
Fuel/Oil Storage
Bassin de Penhoet

FOREWORD

During the interwar period in St. Nazaire, France, the largest dry dock in the world was built. It was 1,150 feet long, 160 feet wide and 50 feet deep. It had been constructed to house the biggest ship in the world, The SS Normandie. Operated by the CGT shipping line, the Normandie entered service in 1935 as the world's largest and fastest passenger liner. Even as she began her working career on the then lucrative transatlantic routes, the storm clouds of war were gathering over Europe....

By 1940 the German military machine had forced France into submission. They occupied the dock at St. Nazaire and began an immediate plan to fortify both it and its approaches. They wanted the facility to be completely safe from seaborne assault and as safe as possible from aerial bombardment. They had big plans for the dock, for it was the only facility outside Germany which could accommodate the Bismarck and Tirpitz battleships. Without St. Nazaire, if these mighty Kriegsmarine capital ships were operating in the North Atlantic and in need of repair, they would be forced to run the gauntlet of the Royal Navy in order to reach home waters....

The gateway to the North Atlantic provided by the Normandie dock offered the Nazis a strategic advantage which was incalculable in terms of its importance; they knew it and the Royal Navy knew it. If the British stood back and did nothing, the Tirpitz and Bismarck would be let loose among the cargo convoys and have a base from which they could be quickly re-fitted if required. In May

1941, the Bismarck was sunk following a daring pursuit by the Royal Navy. She was headed to St. Nazaire after sustaining battle damage during a brief yet devastating sweep of the North Atlantic in which she had sunk the Royal Navy battlecruiser, HMS Hood and seriously damaged HMS Prince of Wales. The loss of the Hood; which for many years had been the most powerful warship afloat, was a severe blow to the morale of the British. By extracting their revenge, the Royal Navy had clawed victory from the jaws of defeat. However, there remained the Tirpitz. If that great warship was able to operate in the open ocean and have a bolt hole in France, the consequences would be dire. For now, Tirpitz was holed up in occupied Norway with her two supporting Kriegsmarine ships, Lutzow and Admiral Scheer….

The Germans knew that the Royal Navy were stretched almost beyond capacity so, if this formidable trio of warships waited long enough, it was likely that Royal Navy vessels assigned to defend against Tirpitz would be dispatched to aid operations in other theatres. Once the British line was weakened, Tirpitz had the perfect opportunity to break out into the North Atlantic, where she, Lutzow and Admiral Scheer could wreak havoc upon the allied convoys which made up the supply lines vital to Britain's survival. If this happened it would mean that the British would almost certainly lose the war….

Meanwhile, safe in the knowledge that they had created an impregnable defence for this most important of docks, the Germans in St. Nazaire were ready and waiting to accept the Tirpitz should she need to be repaired….

On the night of 27th March 1942, the unthinkable happened. The Germans suddenly found themselves under attack from a small flotilla of enemy vessels. How on earth had the Royal Navy managed to penetrate so far inland to attack the dock?

Before they could fully realise the enormity of the situation, British Commandos were ashore in and around the vicinity of the great Normandie dry dock. Operation Chariot had begun....

***

In January 1942, the British Prime Minister, Winston Churchill, wrote a letter to his naval commanders. In it he said. 'The whole strategy of the war turns at this period on this ship....'

If Tirpitz were to join the U-boat fleet in the North Atlantic, then Britain may well be starved into submission. Therefore, it was imperative that she was denied use of the dry dock at St. Nazaire....

The most obvious method of striking the dry dock was from the air. However, the dry dock and the newly constructed U-boat pens nearby were an almost impossible target. A daylight mission, where bombers had the best chance of making a successful strike, was out of the question. The whole area was heavily defended, not only by anti-aircraft artillery, but Luftwaffe fighter Squadrons. Any approach would be met and probably broken up by swarms of BF 109s long before it reached St. Nazaire. The RAF had learned the hard way when it came to deploying its bombers by daylight and had no appetite to repeat their mistakes, even when it came to such critical targets as the Normandie dry dock....

While it was somewhat safer in terms of aircraft survivability, flying by night presented its own unique set of problems. The crudity of aiming and navigation available to the RAF at that point in the war meant that it would be little short of a miracle if even one bomb fell in proximity to its intended target, let alone score a direct hit. Given the need to minimise the potential for civilian casualties in the town which adjoined the docks meant that a night mission was also utterly impractical....

Whilst the dry dock had to be put out of action for as long as possible, it was soon realised the only way to do it was by an attack from the sea....

As already explained, the approaches to the dock had been heavily fortified. The Germans were intent on stopping any threat from the sea....

St. Nazaire is situated on the river Loire, at a point where the river begins to empty into the Loire estuary. The Nazis had approached the problem of protecting St. Nazaire in their usual methodical nature. It was defence in depth. Both banks were teeming with big gun emplacements and powerful searchlights. Further away into the seaward side of the estuary – where it meets the Atlantic – was also bristling with artillery of all calibres. Combined, these guns could put down a devastating pattern of fire across the whole of the approaches to the mouth of the Loire....

Because of the prevalence of shallow water and sand banks, in order to reach the river from the open sea, any approaching vessel would have to follow the one and only main navigation channel. Apart from bringing a vessel close to the northern bank, this would aid the defenders by effectively 'boxing in' any aggressor and leaving him with little scope for manoeuvre. The defending artillery had pre-registered the channel so that they could quickly bring their guns to bear. It was obvious to all that any enemy ship would be sunk before it even reached the mouth of the river....

To add to the problem, the defenders would have ample

notice of the approach of any surface vessel, as they had also sited a radar station where it could sweep the estuary and beyond into the open sea, providing the coastal batteries with early warning of the approach of any hostile craft. Even if it was foggy and no visual contact could be made, working together the radar and artillery were able to direct accurate fire down on any point throughout the whole estuary....

Once – if – an attacking ship made it past the outer ring of defences (which would be nigh impossible) then it would have to face the defences of the port itself. Again, the river was covered by artillery, but now those guns were complimented by fast firing dual purpose anti-aircraft cannons whose barrels could be depressed enough for use in the ground role.

In the highly unlikely event that a ship had made it to within the proximity of the dry dock, how was it to attack? Normal naval guns would do little or no damage to the massive dock gates, and any damage sustained was unlikely to affect their operation. Scuttling the vessel to block the entrance to the dock would only provide the most temporary of solutions. The Germans would have the offending ship raised and removed within a matter of a week or two....

If the dry dock was to be attacked then it would have to be with the intent of rendering it inoperable indefinitely. But how on earth was it to be done...?

***

The problem of how to destroy the dry dock at St. Nazaire was chewed over at great length by various planning committees. Although they attempted to approach the subject from different angles, they all agreed that the operation was impossible. An impatient Churchill was unimpressed by the apparent negativity of his people and remained adamant that the dock could indeed be attacked and destroyed. He wanted the matter resolving in as short a time as possible, before the enemy could put the dry dock into use servicing and repairing the feared Tirpitz and other large Kriegsmarine warships.

Upon the failure of his planners to find a workable solution, he turned the matter over to Combined Operations Headquarters....

Unlike the staid brains of conventional military planners, the Combined Operations staff were an inventive bunch, who approached problems with a different eye. They had their headquarters in London and had been set up shortly after the fall of France in 1940 upon the direct order of Churchill. Their brief was thus; to harass the Germans on the continent of Europe by any means possible. This usually translated into the conducting of pinprick raids against targets of importance by combined Navy and Army units. Perhaps the most high profile action up until that point was Operation Claymore, when a force under Combined Operations command landed on the German held Lofoten Islands in Norway. The primary objective of that raid was to destroy fish oil and glycerine production facilities. Although it may seem innocuous, the fish oil and glycerine was being transported to Germany where it was used in the Nazi war industry for the production of explosives and suchlike. Operation Claymore proved a spectacular success and established proof of concept surrounding the use of small bands of highly trained seaborne troops and aggressive naval vessels to attack the enemy in places he thought himself to be safe....

The troops involved in these actions were no ordinary soldiers, but men from the British Army Commando formations who, in Churchill's own words were 'of the hunter class who can develop a reign of terror down the enemy coast'. Each commando was breed apart, a volunteer who had survived the most physically and mentally exhaustive selection and training the British Army had to offer. Only the best of the best survived commando training and it showed. They were a highly motivated, superbly fit, and expertly trained band of men who were all prepared to undertake the most arduous of taskings....

***

Commander Robert Ryder RN, was a highly experienced and respected officer. He was a recipient of the Polar Medal for pre-war service in the Arctic aboard a Royal Navy research vessel. After the outbreak of hostilities, and whilst on active duty escorting merchant convoys across the dangerous North Atlantic routes, his ship had been torpedoed and sunk by a German U-boat. Commander Ryder survived for four days by clinging to a piece of wood before being rescued by another vessel. His first hand experience meant that Ryder knew only too well the frailties of the convoy system and the overall British inability to adequately defend them against attack. He was also painfully aware of the potential for devastation should Tirpitz be let loose in the convoy lanes between the USA and Britain. In general, convoys were protected by light vessels such as destroyers, corvettes and armed trawlers. If Tirpitz, Lutzow and Admiral Scheer broke into them, there was nothing any convoy escort could do to stop them from sinking every merchant ship they saw....

In late February 1942, Commander Ryder was summoned to London and presented to the Combined Operations planners. He was unaware of the reason for his visit, but was taken aback to find himself in a room full of high ranking officers and the Chief of Combined Operations, Lord Louis Mountbatten. Ryder was ushered to a seat at the conference table around which the others were already seated.

Mountbatten was in the chair and discussing the proposals for an operation against a target of great strategic importance. Mountbatten explained that the Commander Ryder had been selected as naval force commander for the mission and asked if he (Ryder) wished to take on the job. Aware that all eyes were upon him, and still not knowing what he was letting himself in for, Ryder accepted....

Unbeknown to him, the meeting had been in session long before his arrival. The plan had already been worked out and it was here that senior officers had the chance to offer their opinions. They all knew what they were up against and the fantastical nature of the solution which Mountbatten presented to them. Some were enthusiastic, most were sceptical. Mountbatten was quick to point out that, while some of the officers present were convinced that a seaborne attack against such a heavily defended target was impossible, the enemy would also be confident that his precautions were enough to ensure St. Nazaire was immune from surface action. That those in his own command – but more importantly – those in the German command believed that nobody would be foolish enough to attempt such an attack was precisely the reason why it could work....

As the meeting progressed, talk of the operation continued. It quickly became apparent that other avenues had been explored before the task was passed to Combined Operations. As previously mentioned, air attack was already ruled out as unfeasible, as was a stillborn plan to sabotage the dry dock gates by agents of the SOE (Special Operations Executive). The latter was struck off the list simply because of the fact that, aside from the problem of breaching the German defences in and around the harbour then actually approaching the dock gates, the task of destroying them would take time; some hours in fact, and would require far more explosives than a few saboteurs could ever hope to carry....

Although he had no need to, Mountbatten impressed the importance of the Normandie dock for the Nazi war effort upon his planning team. To attack and destroy the target was of the utmost priority, this was the order of the Prime Minister, and that is why this most unusual and dangerous of plans was being put into action....

***

After the meeting was concluded, and during the return journey to his home base, Ryder's mind was awash with what Combined Operations were proposing. Their plan was simply outrageous! He (Ryder) was to lead a small flotilla of vessels, aboard which would be a unit of the crack British commandos, to attack the German naval installation at St. Nazaire and destroy the dry dock and its ancillary equipment. He had been told that St. Nazaire was the most heavily defended Kriegsmarine base in France, that the mission was fraught with danger and the likelihood of survival slender. Still, and despite the unusually high risks involved; risks which even in wartime would have meant the mission would not be approved, Ryder took to his task with typical determination....

The plan itself, as presented by Mountbatten, was simple. Ryder was to take an old destroyer which had been laden with high explosive, sail her from Falmouth the 450 miles to St. Nazaire, somehow evading the Luftwaffe and roving Kriegsmarine surface ships and submarines, past the German defences in the Loire estuary and ram her into the gates of the dry dock. Thereafter, the commandos on the ship and the accompanying small boats, would land and attack several key facilities vital to the operation of the dry dock. They would then embark upon the boats and withdraw. The apparent simplicity of the proposal failed to underscore the enormous physical dangers involved. Ryder wondered if the planners had taken into account what the Germans would be doing during this time. Indeed, it appeared that the enemy response was mostly left to the imagination....

Assuming the raiding force made it to the Normandie dry dock and rammed the gates, the Royal Navy had another surprise for the enemy. The destroyer was to be fitted with an enormous explosive charge. After the withdrawal, this delayed action bomb would activate, blowing the ship to kingdom come and taking the dry dock gates with it. It was calculated that the sheer force of the blast would render the dry dock inoperable for at least a year, thus forcing the Tirpitz to use the only bases capable of accommodating her, and those were in Germany....

Trying to reach the North Atlantic from Germany meant that Tirpitz had only three routes available, through the English Channel, between Scotland and Iceland or the Denmark straits. All were perilous, as they were covered by aircraft and strong Royal Navy forces. Of the three, the channel route was an option which was the least realistic. While the Luftwaffe could provide strong air cover, if the Tirpitz tried to break out via the Channel she would be attacked mercilessly by the RAF and Royal Navy, and at one point would even be within range of shore based anti-shipping guns on the Kent coast. The remaining two routes meant she had a far better chance of breaking through into the convoy lanes, but if she sustained damage she would be forced to try and fight her way back home without support against an enemy who would descend quickly and in strength to finish her off. The fate of the Bismarck had forced the Kriegsmarine to be unusually cautious with their prize warship. The British were confident that the enemy wouldn't risk her out in the open ocean if she didn't have a port to which she could easily retire. So, by destroying the dry dock gates at St. Nazaire, Tirpitz would be effectively removed from the battle of the Atlantic.

Ryder knew the importance of the dry dock, and the effect its loss would have on Kriegsmarine operations in the battle of the Atlantic, but he also knew that there was no way any British ship could run the gauntlet of German defences which protected St. Nazaire and its dry dock. So, in order to survive long enough to make the attack, he and the Royal Navy would use guile instead of strength....

***

HMS Campbeltown was an elderly warship. She had been launched in 1919 then taken into service with the United States Navy as the USS Buchanan. She was one of fifty such vessels which had been handed over to the Royal Navy by the American government as part of the 'lease lend' programme. She was tired and hardly up to the task of modern naval warfare, therefore her loss on a one way 'suicide' mission would have no impact upon the wider operational capabilities of the Royal Navy....

Once 'Operation Chariot' had been given the necessary approval, Campbeltown was removed from general service sailed into Devonport where the Royal Navy set about a feverish programme of adaptation to prepare her for her final voyage.

The impossibility of sailing Campbeltown along the only navigable channel in the Loire estuary, danger close to the northern shore, in the face of enemy artillery stationed along it meant that another, altogether more daring approach was needed....

After lengthy debate as to the feasibility of such a move, it was decided to take Campbeltown across the shallows and sandbanks where she would stand a better chance of survival. This in itself was a high risk strategy, for the water through which she was expected to sail was dangerously shallow. Indeed, even during the high Spring tides in which the operation had been scheduled to take place, in parts there would as little as twenty four inches between the keel and the sea bed. If Campbeltown became stuck at any time during her approach then not only would she face certain destruction by German artillery, but the whole operation would fail....

In order to lessen the chance of the Campbeltown grounding herself, the Royal Navy team assigned to prepare her for the mission began to systematically strip her of all excess weight. The main guns, torpedo tubes and depth charge systems were removed and replaced by 20mm Oerlikon cannons, a quick firing 76mm gun and some .50 calibre machineguns. Everything below deck was unbolted or cut away and taken ashore, leaving the ship completely devoid of internal fittings. One of her boilers was removed and she would only carry enough fuel to reach the dry dock....

As a result of such drastic alteration, Campbeltown began to rise in the water. Her ability to manoeuvre and sail in anything but calm weather was compromised and all involved knew she would be prone to capsize in heavy seas; still, nothing else could be done to ensure that she made it across the shallows and on to the target....

Despite the draconian measures taken to lighten her, it was deemed necessary to protect the bridge, wheelhouse and areas of the deck from the incoming fire to which everyone concerned knew the ship would be subjected. To that end, armour plate was fitted at these vital points. With one eye firmly on the weight situation, 4.5 tons of amatol high explosive was placed in the bowels of the Campbeltown, underneath the pedestal where her forward gun had been. It was a fine balance between weight and explosive power. After much deliberation, the experts considered this enough to wreck the heavy dry dock gates but not enough to cause issues when crossing the sandbanks....

The Royal Navy didn't restrict itself to stripping and refitting the Campbeltown. Other, equally drastic measures were taken to afford her a degree of protection....

In profile, the old ship looked like what she was; an obsolete allied destroyer. Even in the darkness any Germans seeing the Campbeltown in profile would recognise her lines then raise the alarm and direct fire onto her. What if the British could fool the enemy long enough to allow Campbeltown passage through the estuary? If the Germans thought that this mysterious ship which had suddenly turned up in the Loire estuary at night was one of their own then in all likelihood they would hold their fire. The British knew they wouldn't be able to fool the enemy for long, but perhaps just long enough to get her past the guns and on to the dry dock...?

To this end, work to alter the appearance of Campbeltown and make her look like a Kriegsmarine vessel was started. Because of the loss of the boiler, the rearmost pair of her four funnels were now redundant. They were removed and the voids capped. The remaining two were then cut at an angle to resemble those typical of German destroyers. Once spotted on radar then illuminated by searchlight or flares from the shore batteries, it was hoped that the defenders would be confused enough to buy the raiders time.

As well as looking similar to a friendly ship, she would also by flying the Kriegsmarine flag; although considered 'ungentlemanly' by some, this was a perfectly legitimate ruse de guerre just so long as it was struck when the shooting started….

As soon as she was spotted in the estuary, the British knew the Campbeltown would be challenged, not by gunfire but a request that she identify herself. This is where the British had an ace up their sleeve….

Bletchley Park was home to the British code breaking effort. The Germans used a system called 'Enigma', a highly sophisticated method of encoding radio traffic which was then passed via Morse code signalling.

The Germans considered Enigma to be unbreakable, but the staff at Bletchley has indeed broken the Enigma codes, not only had they broken them, but so decisively that they could read messages almost as quickly as they were being passed among the enemy….

For some weeks Bletchley had been under orders to pay particular attention to the radio traffic emanating from around the St. Nazaire area. What they discovered was of incalculable importance, and would make the difference between the Campbeltown being quickly attacked, or given time to pass under the noses of the defenders….

As well as help from Bletchley to discover the location of minefields protecting the estuary and the sea lane through them, the British were also in possession of one of the latest Kriegsmarine code books. The book in question was captured during an earlier commando raid against the island of Vaagso in Nazi occupied Norway. This book contained all the signals which any German military vessel would use in order to satisfy the shore batteries that they were dealing with a friendly ship....

After being tracked on radar to a point where she was in sight of land, the Germans would demand to know who the Campbeltown was. If she failed to comply with their request then the now alerted shore batteries would open fire. The challenge would not be made by radio, but signal lamp. The Germans would ask for the ship to identify that she was friendly in order for them to allow her to pass. Once the challenge was made, Campbeltown would use her Aldis lamp to flash the correct recognition code. To back this up, the flotilla was also in possession of the pattern of coloured flares which could be fired into the night sky to further satisfy a suspicious enemy....

Of course, those who were charged with conducting the raid would never know how the Royal Navy had come into possession of these secret German signal codes, probably assuming they had been found out from captured Kriegsmarine officers. The fact was that such codes were changed regularly in order to thwart any intelligence the British may have come into possession of. That notice of the change of codes were transmitted to those concerned via the 'unbreakable' Enigma, meant that Bletchley had been able to supply the task force with very latest information. Indeed, the flare pattern which would allow entry into the estuary had only been changed a matter of days before the operation was launched. This would further help the Campbeltown, as the enemy would never suspect that the British had access to them....

Campbeltown would not be alone on her mission. She was to be at the head of a force of other Royal Navy vessels. Whilst the small boats which were to accompany her could easily negotiate the shallow waters of the estuary, they had their own potentially devastating problems to deal with. They were of the ML (Motor Launch) class. Small, fast and manoeuvrable, these boats had quickly proved their worth in several roles. However, they shared one potentially lethal flaw; they traded speed and manoeuvrability for armour. In fact there was no armour almost anywhere at all on these craft. As amazing as it sounds they were constructed almost exclusively from wood. The engines were petrol powered and the fuel tanks barely able to stop a rifle bullet. To take a round in the fuel tanks would cause fire and probable explosion. To make matters worse, they were possessed of short range. To get them the 450 miles to St. Nazaire and back, each boat would have to carry extra fuel. There was nowhere to mount long range tanks other than the decks. The need for speed and the fact that there were simply no armoured tanks available meant the boats would have to go into action with the increased risk that their extra cargo of highly flammable petrol would be hit by enemy fire….

Like Campbeltown, the MLs were adapted for the mission. Aside from the deck mounted long range fuel tanks, the obsolete Hotchkiss three pounder gun mounted on foredeck of each boat was removed and replaced by the reliable Oerlikon 20mm cannon. The Oerlikon was a hard hitting weapon which could be used in both the air defence and ground roles and would provide the MLs with increased firepower. Two Vickers machineguns were mounted to either side of the bridge. Aft, another 'bandstand' mounted Oerlikon and twin Lewis machineguns were already fitted to the craft as part of its normal armament.

The MLs were never intended to be used in the role which they had now been given. However, it was hoped that this new weapons fit would allow the ML gunners some semblance of effectiveness when engaging the concentrated German shore defences....

The MLs job was to ferry the commandos to the start positions for their attacks then lift them off the docks and speed them and the Campbeltown's crew out of the estuary to safety.

A Motor Gun Boat (MGB 314) was to act as the command vessel, carrying amongst others, Commander Ryder and the ground force officer in charge, Lieutenant-Colonel Charles Newman.

The last boat was a Motor Torpedo Boat (MTB 74). Both MGB 314 and MTB 74 were constructed using the same materials as the MLs and therefore very vulnerable to enemy fire.

MTB 74 had her own tasking. She would follow the Campbeltown and, in the event of her missing the dry dock gates or being sunk before she reached them, MTB 74 was to position herself then fire two delayed action torpedoes into the gates. Like the MLs, she had been adapted for her mission specific role. Her 18 inch diameter torpedo tubes had been repositioned from the centre of the boat to her bow so the torpedoes would 'swim' to their target at a shallower depth than normal, allowing them to pass over the anti-torpedo nets which protected the approaches to the dry dock. The effectiveness of this attack was open to question. The dock gates were thirty-six feet thick. Any hope that they would be destroyed by a couple of torpedoes was, at best, wishful thinking....

If Campbeltown managed to strike the dock gates as planned, then MTB 74 had a secondary mission. She was to close on the old entrance to the 'Bassin de St. Nazaire', the inner basin next to the main dry dock, where another pair of gates were positioned and fire her torpedoes into them. The plan was that, once they hit, the torpedoes would sink to the base of the gates and remain there until they exploded (at roughly the same time as the

Campbeltown's own charge was timed to go off), destroying the gates and the ability to control water flow into the basin. This was important as it would disrupt the operation of the main part of the harbour and movements of U-boats entering or leaving the recently built maintenance pens....

***

As touched upon earlier, although the dry dock was the primary target, it was realised that the opportunity to destroy as much critical equipment as possible around the docks themselves was not to be missed. The commandos took to their tasking with typical relish....

Lieutenant-Colonel Charles Newman was a superb officer who had served with the British Special Service Brigade since its formation. His men held him in the highest regard. Known simply as 'Colonel Charles', he was a mild mannered but tough man whom the commandos would follow wherever he led.

The commando units which made up the brigade were the cream of the British Army and the envy of friend and foe alike. They had been engaged in many daring operations but 'Operation Chariot', was to be like no other....

Liaising with his second in command for the mission, Major Bill Copland, Lieutenant-Colonel Newman had first spoken of 'an important job'. Without giving any detail, he instructed the Major to pick 173 men from Number 2 Commando and put them through a period of intensive training in street fighting at night. They were joined by 92 men from other commando units who the Special Service Brigade HQ wanted to go on the mission.

Together they were to be drilled relentlessly until the skills required were instinctive.

Major Copland was told he had only a few weeks to get his men into the state of readiness required. The motto for this regime was simple; 'Night, night, night. Street, fight, fight!'....

The immediate problem for Major Copland was not who he should choose, but who he should leave out. He knew that every single man under his command in 2 Commando was a superb soldier. Highly trained, disciplined and self reliant, the commandos were 'men amongst men'. Indeed, they were so professional that each one could easily have made senior NCO ranks in other units.

Carefully, Copland chose his team and introduced them immediately to an exhaustive programme of training....

Street fighting is the most arduous and dangerous of all infantry skills and the most difficult to master. Using live ammunition, grenades and explosives, the commandos were put through their paces at night in evacuated areas of city suburbs where bombed out buildings and rubble littered the landscape.

The heavy noise created by the commandos soon caused issues with the locals who lived within earshot of the places the army had chosen to train. Many complaints were made to the police but were fielded with the same response. It was a military matter, and as such beyond civil police jurisdiction. This prompted further complaints to the local military authorities. Apologies for the inconvenience given and concerned civilians assured that the disruption would not last long....

In the meantime, just as they were promised by Major Copland, officers and other ranks alike were worked almost to a standstill. Soon they were expert in the technicalities of urban warfare and building clearing.

However, they continued to work blind. Nobody knew the reason behind all this training and all were too clever to ask. Each man was sure that they were being readied for an operation somewhere in occupied Europe. They didn't care where and had little regard for the risks; they just wanted to get to grips with the enemy....

The Combined Operations planners had identified several key installations which were each vital to the operation of the dry dock and neighbouring basin. Lieutenant-Colonel Newman was still the only man in his team to know the detail of the mission. He also knew that the immediate area surrounding the dry dock was heavily guarded by German troops who in turn were supported by machinegun emplacements and anti-aircraft cannon....

As the Campbeltown made her final approach, it was assumed that her disguise had been seen through and the garrison alerted. Taking fire from numerous points in and around the dry dock, it would be an exceptionally difficult task for the commandos to disembark and deploy to their respective targets, let alone actually attack them. Campbeltown would be steaming at full speed as she struck the dock gates and the impact would be enough to throw those onboard into disarray. It was imperative that the commandos were able to get ashore without delay. The thickness of the gates meant there was no way the old destroyer could hope to breach them, instead it was expected that she would simply imbed herself into them, stoving in the bow and placing the hidden explosives tight up against the target. The commandos would not only have to be prepared for the almighty collision, but able to quickly deploy....

Lieutenant-Colonel Newman knew his men would have to be off and away from the Campbeltown the moment she hit, otherwise they would be caught in a wall of crossfire from German strongpoints sited in the vicinity of the dry dock. To this end, and expecting the worst, he had ordered that ladders and climbing ropes be stowed on the Campbeltown's deck; this would allow rapid debarkation of the commandos to their respective assembly points.

It was all about speed; his men must move quickly away from the ship and get to grips with the defenders. There would be no time for stand up firefights, it was imperative that his men fight through the opposition and close on their targets before the enemy had chance to organise themselves and react to the attack. On this particular point, Lieutenant-Colonel Newman was confident his commandos held the advantage. As well as being supremely fit, exceptionally well trained, and in most cases battle hardened, they were also possessed of an aggressive fighting spirit which the enemy would find very difficult to counter. They would keep going forward, regardless of the odds, until they had killed, captured or driven off the Germans and reached their objectives....

Although relatively lightly equipped, each man was well armed. Most of them were carrying the formidable Thompson submachine gun. This American designed and manufactured weapon was a favourite amongst the commando formation. It was handy, reliable and; firing the heavy .45 bullet, very hard hitting. The commandos were masters of this weapon, able to shoot accurately from any position. They were taught to fire from the hip while advancing, and as a result could lay down murderous fire on the move. To provide more firepower, the Bren light machinegun would also feature in the commando arsenal. The Bren was a much loved weapon with the British for the same reasons as the Thompson. Firing the .303 round, the Bren had the ability to engage the enemy at long ranges, an important consideration if the raiders were to stand any chance of suppressing German positions beyond the target area....

Aside from the men on the Campbeltown, other teams of commandos were to be simultaneously landed by ML across the rest of the docks. Although their overall numbers were small and they would be hopelessly outnumbered, the commandos knew that to hit the enemy in several areas at once would help to create panic and confusion among those who were guarding the facilities and create the impression that they were under attack from a much larger force. This confusion would pass, and pass quickly, but the men knew that while it lasted it would hopefully allow them time to accomplish their mission....

The huge pumps which filled and emptied the dry dock, electric motors and winding gear which powered them were to be destroyed as part of the primary objectives. These particular targets were known to the commandos as 'critical points', equipment which was vital to the operation of the dry dock. Even if the gates themselves remained intact, the removal of the pumps and motors would mean that the ability to operate the dry dock would be fatally compromised. The damage done could be repaired of course, but it would be both costly and time consuming and while the dock remained out of commission, so too did the threat of the Tirpitz....

Captain Bill Pritchard of the Royal Engineers and his second in command, Captain Bob Montgomery, were assigned to lead a team of commandos in the attack against these targets. Pritchard had been training his men hard ever since he had been given his tasking. They trained day and night at the dry docks at Southampton and Cardiff, where equipment similar to that in St. Nazaire was to be found. The King George V dry dock at Southampton was of particular use to Pritchard's team as it was the one which most closely resembled the target. It was a massive facility, big enough to hold the 75000 ton 'Queen Mary' passenger liner.

Having full run of the dry dock, and drawing on the expertise of its engineers, the commandos learned where to place the explosive charges to create maximum damage.

Each of the pumps, electric motors and winding gears were to be targeted at the same point. Just fixing explosives could well mean that the enemy might be able to cannibalise some of the machinery to make the rest work, by blowing them up at the same points meant that this would be impossible.

During the training the teams were rotated, so those assigned the pumping equipment trained to attack the electric motors or winding gear and vice versa. If any of the teams were unable to complete their tasking, after dealing with their own targets the others could quickly step in and take their place.

To ensure that there was as little room for error as possible, they often worked in complete darkness, sometimes even blindfolded so that setting the explosives in the correct place became instinctive....

Once the training had ended, each man in the demolitions teams knew how to destroy all of this critical machinery and could do so quickly and with flawless accuracy. This was considered essential as once on the ground, anything could happen....

The dry dock and its associated equipment wasn't the only target. There was a large underground oil storage depot sited immediately beside eastern edge of the dry dock. This facility held millions of gallons of fuel oil and diesel which the Nazis were using to replenish ships and U-boats; as such it was an important target which – if destroyed – would also heavily impact the day to day operation of the St. Nazaire docks. There were also some smaller targets which the other raiding teams would attend to such as railway lines, rolling stock, locomotives and cranes. Through intelligence reports and intercepts from Bletchley, the planners also knew that there were numerous Kriegsmarine vessels moored in the St. Nazaire and Penhoet basins which adjoined the Normandie dry dock. These too would become targets for the commandos....

While the commandos were ashore the Royal Navy were to attack any shipping found in the river. Unfortunately the newly constructed U-boat pens were situated on the landward side of the main Bassin de St. Nazaire and as such, were beyond the reach of the flotilla. Immune to air attack, the massive concrete structure was responsible for the repair and refitting of the deadly German submarines which stalked the convoy routes of the North Atlantic. It was a bitter pill to swallow, but this important Nazi facility would remain untouched....

The commandos were divided into three groups. Groups No.1 and 2 were to be taken into action aboard the MLs, while the third group were on Campbeltown.

Group No.1 were to deal with enemy defences on a pier known as 'the old mole'. It was vital that this primary target was taken then held as it was earmarked as the embarkation point for the whole raiding force during their withdrawal. Like other places of importance in and around the docks, it was well guarded. Attached to the mole was a slipway, and it was here that the commandos planned to land, right under the noses of the German defenders.

After subduing the enemy on the mole, the commandoes were to attack and destroy anti-aircraft emplacements sited close by. This was to be achieved with all speed as the guns could be depressed and used in the ground role so, as such; they posed an immediate threat to the vulnerable MLs.

Their mission didn't end there. They were then to move inland to the old town, fighting through the German defences as they went. They had been ordered to blow up the power station. Moving west for a short distance would bring them to the 'south lock'. Once there, all bridges within their sector and the lock gates at the new entrance to the Bassin de St. Nazaire were to be demolished. The removal of these gates, along with the torpedoing of the old ones by MTB 74 would ensure that any shipping; but especially the U-boats trying to reach the pens, would be prevented from entering the basin....

Group No.2 was to be landed at the old entrance to the basin, close to the Normandie dry dock.. They would then spread out to attack anti-aircraft guns, the German headquarters and the old lock gates. Their job thereafter was to protect Group N0.3 against counter attack or anti-aircraft fire from positions at the U-boat pens....

The objectives of Group No.3 has already been explained. They would be aboard the Campbeltown and from there would attack their own targets....

Because of the amount of explosives required to carry out the various demolitions, even the ultra fit commandos would struggle to carry them and other equipment. To this end it was decided that the demolition party members would only be armed with pistols. They were to be defended by protection teams, whose job was to clear the way to the targets then make sure that the demolitions teams weren't attacked while they went about their taskings. After the explosives had been placed, the demolitions teams were instructed to arm themselves with weaponry from dead Germans (of whom they assured would be many). They could then join in the fighting alongside the other commandos. Because of their role in attacking targets in Nazi occupied territory, all commandos were trained to use enemy small arms and thus were as proficient in their use as their own rifles and sub-machineguns.

***

Lieutenant-Commander Stephen Beattie (known as 'Sam') took over command of HMS Campbeltown only a couple of weeks before Operation Chariot was scheduled to take place.

The old ship was still in the middle of its refit when he arrived. As soon as the ship was ready, Beattie took her out into the English Channel for a series of short sea trials. Concerned that the handling properties of Campbeltown had been compromised, he wanted to familiarise himself with the way she reacted under various circumstances. It was a prudent move. As already predicted, the loss in weight meant that the ship was sluggish in manoeuvre and therefore the ability to make the necessary quick turns needed to bring the ship to bear on the dock gates within the confines of the waters surrounding it were all but impossible. Beattie knew he would have only one chance to turn Campbeltown onto its target so it was vital that he could accurate steer her. However, he realised that while travelling at 17 knots and above, the handling corrected itself to a point where it became acceptable. This then, Beattie concluded, was the minimum speed at which the ship would make its approach....

The main explosive charge which was to destroy the target consisted of twenty four depth charges, in six sections, each encased in concrete and steel, as well as the reason described in the next paragraph, the concrete and metal would serve to hide them from view in case the enemy managed to board the ship after the raid had ended. The fuse which would detonate the explosives after a time delay of two hours, was itself carefully hidden in the leg of a mess room table. It was hoped that if the Germans spotted the concrete, they would conclude that it was an attempt to strengthen the bow of the Campbeltown for her ramming attack....

This mighty explosive device was the brainchild of Lieutenant Nigel Tibbits, a brilliant Royal Navy demolitions expert. He knew the pressing need to keep the weight of explosives down to the bare minimum required to destroy the heavy dock gates. He also knew how to do the job with less explosives than otherwise be deemed necessary. The trick was to successfully direct the explosive force contained within the charges, thus enabling them to punch through the target. The charges had been placed far enough back from the bow to take account of the enormous damage expected to occur when Campbeltown hit the dock gates. Tibbits had calculated the point where, after she had come to rest, the explosives would be directly on top of the target. The concrete and steel casing would direct the blast downwards in a narrow arc and directly into the dock gates, the energy contained within the explosion would have nowhere to go except where Tibbits wanted it to and such would be its force that Lieutenant Tibbits knew it would demolish the target with such violence that it would be rendered beyond repair....

***

Preparations for the mission continued apace. Time was short and the need to take advantage of the spring tides vital....

The actual attack phase of Operation Chariot was not the only concern of Combined Operations. How could they expect to sail the force from the UK to St. Nazaire without being spotted? The seas around the coast of France were heavily patrolled by the Luftwaffe and these patrols were supplemented by those of the Kriegsmarine, so it wasn't a question of not being seen but more of how to fool the enemy into thinking that this small flotilla was doing something else and posed no threat to the Loire estuary...?

Campbeltown and the small boats were to be joined for the voyage by the Royal Navy destroyers HMS Atherstone and Tynedale. These ships were to provide an escort to the vulnerable Campbeltown but were to remain out at sea while the attack took place. The planners decided to organise the flotilla into the formation used by the Royal Navy when conducting anti-submarine sweeps. The Germans were familiar with this particular formation as they were often seen on the main shipping routes. So, it was hoped the raiders would be mistaken for one of these regular sorties on their way from the UK to Gibraltar. Because – primarily for safety reasons – they had not been fitted with the long range fuel tanks found on the other MLs, MGB 314 (the command boat) and MTB 74 would be taken under tow by the Atherstone and Campbeltown respectively until they were within range of the Loire estuary. After the attack had taken place the surviving MLs would rendezvous with the destroyers for the return journey....

Everyone knew that an enraged enemy would be out to get them and all concerned expected the ships to be subjected to fierce air attack as well as possible submarine and surface vessel action. They could expect no support from their own side. They would be beyond RAF fighter range for much of the voyage and the Navy would not dispatch other warships to help with their defence. They would simply have to fight their way home through everything the Nazis would throw at them....

***

Soon the preparations were complete. The Campbeltown and small boats were assembled at Falmouth then given orders to prepare to sail at short notice. The commandos arrived and set about readying themselves. Weapons were cleaned then double checked and kit prepared....

Even for the busy Falmouth docks, the unusual flurry of activity surrounding the appearance of Campbeltown and the MLs, coupled with the sudden arrival of commandos were bound to set tongues wagging. For the benefit of the workers and any Nazi spies, it was made known that they were the '10th Anti-Submarine Striking Force', a wholly fictitious unit whose job was to hunt down Nazi U-boats on the western approaches. For now though, the '10th Anti-Submarine Striking Force' was to be deployed to the Mediterranean, sailing to that theatre via Gibraltar.

For the benefit of any watching fifth column, sun helmets and other hot weather gear was openly taken aboard the ships in an effort to convince them that this indeed was the case....

Lord Mountbatten called Lieutenant-Colonel Newman and told him that, because of the exceptional difficulty and danger they were about to face, Combined Operations were writing him and his men off. "I'm confident." Mountbatten said. "That you can get and do the job, but we cannot hold out much hope of you getting out again. Even if you are all lost, the results of the operation will have been worth it. For that reason I want you to tell all the men who have family responsibilities, or who think they should stand down for any reason, that they are free to do so, and nobody will think any worse of them."

Lieutenant-Colonel Newman assembled his men on the

eve of the operation and passed on Mountbatten's words. He added that, as far as the commandos were concerned, no shame would be attached to any man not wishing to participate and they could continue to serve with the commando formations without a stain on their character or record.

The men listened intently. What was said to them was unique. Never before or again would British soldiers be given such a choice. When the Colonel had finished not one man stood down. They were all raring to go. The fact that many were likely not to return did nothing to dampen their determination to see the mission through to its conclusion. If anyone could turn the massive odds which were against them in their favour, it was the commando....

The latest aerial reconnaissance photos delivered to Combined Operations HQ did make for good viewing. RAF photographic interpreters had uncovered some significant and potentially devastating changes in and around St. Nazaire and the Loire estuary since Operation Chariot had been given the go ahead....

Several new heavy guns had been positioned on the approaches to the port to bolster the already formidable firepower available to the Germans.

Aside from ten minesweepers moored in the Bassin de St. Nazaire (which all carried deck armament that could be used against the commandos once they were ashore). Four harbour defence boats had also been spotted. The British would have no way of knowing if these boats would be out on patrol around the docks or in the estuary itself at the time of the attack. If any where then they could create serious problems for the British force.

The photographs also revealed four motor torpedo boats of the Möwe class tied up at the old entrance, next to the Normandie dock. Ironically, these craft were moored in exactly the same spot where the second commando group intended to come ashore....

These changes were of great concern to Mountbatten and his team because they meant the raiding force would now face even more opposition than planned. The findings were communicated to both Commander Ryder and Lieutenant-Colonel Newman, along with the instruction that the mission would still go ahead.

It was hoped that most of the moored enemy craft would be only manned by skeleton crews and thus unable to engage the British. Using their own deck armament, the MLs might be able to dispatch the torpedo boats before they were able to enter into the fight....

When the order to begin the operation was received the commandos were embarked and the vessels readied for the off. Once out at sea, the commandos on the deck of HMS Campbeltown were to don Royal Navy issue duffle coats over their uniforms so that if the flotilla was spotted by submarine or low flying reconnaissance aircraft, they would be taken for sailors....

At the very last moment four MLs from the 20th and 28th Motor Launch flotillas were attached to the main force. They had been fitted with four torpedo tubes each. Their primary mission was not to participate in the attack but provide extra protection should the flotilla run into opposition from the Kriegsmarine on the outward journey.

As last minute preparations were being made, those manning MTB 74 (the boat tasked with torpedoing either the main dry dock gates or the gates to the old entrance to the Bassin de St. Nazaire) had a problem. The delayed action fuses which were meant to be fitted to their torpedoes had not arrived. MTB 74s skipper, Sub-Lieutenant Michael Wynn, knew that if he mentioned the fact to those in authority his boat would be scrubbed from the operation. He told his crew not to tell anyone who happened to ask that MTB 74 wasn't ready while waiting in the hope that those damned fuses would arrive before it was too late….

***

Finally, the flotilla set off from Falmouth, Cornwall, at 1400hrs on the 26th March 1942. Instead of being forced to tell his commanders of the fuse situation and being removed from the raiding force, Sub-Lieutenant Wynn's patience paid off. Only fifteen minutes before they were due to depart, the long overdue fuses had arrived at the dockside. Still keeping quiet about his close shave, Wynn ordered his crew to fit them while at sea….

For the first leg of the journey, the flotilla enjoyed air cover but soon they were out of range of friendly fighters. Anything they saw in the sky thereafter was bound to be hostile. They were aware that the Luftwaffe paid particular attention to this part of the ocean, as it was used regularly for convoy movements between the UK and Gibraltar, or by those ships making the long journey around the Cape of Good Hope to the middle and Far East.

U-boats, some of whom were based in St. Nazaire, also stalked the area looking for prey. As soon as they were spotted by aerial reconnaissance, surface vessels or submarines, the raiders knew they could expect trouble….

Ironically, on the same day as the Campbeltown set sail, the Kriegsmarine Commander in Chief, Admiral Karl Doenitz, arrived in St. Nazaire for an inspection of the port and the new U-boat pens. Doenitz knew the strategic importance of the Normandie dry dock and asked the local commander about the defences and if the British would be able to attack it from the sea. Doenitz was assured that, because of the strength of the coastal batteries and the fact that the only navigation channel was so close to the guns, any attack would be simply impossible....

Once safely at sea the sailors were finally told the detail of their mission. They were under no illusion that Operation Chariot was likely to be a one way trip, and that many of them would be killed or captured. Still, not a single man wavered at the prospect of what they were to face....

Although he had finally armed his two torpedoes, Sub-Lieutenant Wynn had other problems to contend with. MTB 74 was an 'eccentric' vessel, almost possessed with a mind of her own. She was powered by five large petrol engines which endowed her with terrific speed. However, at least one of the engines seemed always to be unserviceable. The biggest issue was the fact that – regardless of where the throttles were set – the engines often only seemed to operate on two settings; idle or flank speed. Nobody could ever get to the bottom of why she misbehaved in such a manner, but Wynn knew it may well prove problematic during the approach and attack phases of the mission. The Naval Force commander, Robert Ryder, was well aware of MTB 74s failings and had taken her off the operation, only for Wynn to present himself and plead so eloquently for the chance to take part that she was reinstated....

During the voyage to the target area, being towed by Campbeltown, all was well but once under her own steam anything could happen. Wynn could call for 'full speed ahead' only to find the boat bobbing ineffectually in the water. Conversely, when stealth was required she might go racing off at 40 knots. Once in the Loire estuary, any high speeds would be sure to put the Germans on high alert and possibly blow Campbeltown's cover before she could reach the mouth of the river. Once at the target (if she reached the target!) Wynn's problems were magnified. If MTB 74 chose to misbehave he might find himself running at top speed within the combat area and unable to manoeuvre effectively enough to bring his torpedoes to bear on what then would become an impossibly small target. At the other end of the scale, MTB 74 might just decide she didn't want to play anymore and bring herself to a standstill, if that was the case she would be quickly caught in the enemy searchlights and illumination flares then raked with fire....

The convoy sailed on, passing dangerously close to Brest. It was at around this time that they encountered a sizable fleet of French fishing boats. Unsure if they were innocent civilian fishermen or Nazi spy vessels, Ryder ordered two of the boats to be boarded. The crews were removed to one of the destroyers and their boats sank. The Frenchmen insisted that, as far as they knew, there were no enemy spies aboard the remaining trawlers. Commander Ryder decided to leave the rest of the fleet alone and take the chance that the composition, course and speed of his flotilla would not be reported to the enemy.

Later that same day a coded signal from Royal Navy headquarters informed Ryder that Kriegsmarine E-boats had been spotted by an RAF reconnaissance aircraft to the south of the flotilla. The E-boat (known as 'Schnellboot' or 'S-boot' to the Germans) was a well armed vessel in a similar class to the British MTB. As the German name suggested, it was fast and capable of speeds up to 48 knots. It had several key advantages over its British counterparts. It could travel long distances without carrying extra fuel, was better handling at sea and, crucially, had far superior protection from enemy fire than the Flimsy MTB....

Ryder knew that if the E-boats managed to intercept his ships he would be in serious trouble. They would make fast torpedo attacks against the Campbeltown and her accompanying destroyers. Whilst the Atherton and Tyneside could possibly manoeuvre their way out of trouble, for the sluggish Campbeltown, it would be a different matter. If his hunch about the innocence of those French fishing crews proved wrong, then the heading of his force would have been telegraphed to the mainland and then relayed to the E-boats. They were sure to be attacked.

The gravity of the situation was acknowledged back in the UK. Ryder was further informed that another pair of destroyers had been dispatched to provide extra protection. HMS Brocklesby and HMS Cleveland were sailing at full speed and would join Ryder's flotilla in the coming hours....

Though the overcast conditions meant that the convoy had seen no sign of the Luftwaffe, Kriegsmarine activity was still a great concern. Although the expected E-boat attack never materialised, the convoy was spotted by a surfaced U-boat operating out of St. Nazaire. In turn the submarine was sighted then attacked with depth charges by HMS Atherton after it crash dived. The U-boat survived and, at the first opportunity, reported the action. It told regional Kriegsmarine command that the British ships it had encountered were an anti-submarine patrol sailing to Gibraltar. The ruse had worked!

***

Eventually, after dark, the flotilla came to within 75 miles of the target. Atherton, Tyneside and the four torpedo armed MLs sheared off. As a feint they were to continue steaming towards Gibraltar until the time the attack on St. Nazaire was scheduled to take place. They would then come about and return to a point off the Loire estuary where they intended to rendezvous with the destroyers Brocklesby and Cleveland to await the return of the raiding force....

It was time for the attacking force to change formation. In the vanguard was the headquarters boat, MGB 314 with Ryder and Newman aboard. She was flanked by a couple of MLs with Campbeltown and the rest of the boats following on....

In order to bring the flotilla to the correct point at the mouth of the Loire estuary, a British submarine was waiting to guide them in. HMS Sturgeon had been sitting on the seabed ever since the attackers left Falmouth. Surfacing now, but using her radio navigation beacon carefully so it transmitted a narrow beam out to sea, she was able to remain undetected by listening posts along the banks of the Loire. The flotilla tuned their specially fitted navigation receivers into the Sturgeon's signal and began to ride the beam all the way to the point of entry to the estuary. HMS Sturgeon's role was vital to the mission, as even a minor navigational error could see Campbeltown sailing too close to the coast or running aground on some of the none navigable areas of the estuary....

As Campbeltown closed on the Sturgeon she raised the Kriegsmarine flag. Looking out from the bridge, Campbeltown's Captain, Lieutenant-Commander Beattie, studied the scene before him. In the far distance he could make out the beams of searchlights playing across the night sky and the flash of anti-aircraft shells exploding over St. Nazaire. He knew that the RAF had arrived....

With only RAF Top Brass knowing why, Bomber

Command had been ordered to attack St. Nazaire. They were to do so regardless of weather conditions and other factors which might normally see a sortie cancelled. They just knew they were to arrive at 23.30 hours and remain for one hour. Although resources were stretched, the RAF committed sixty-two aircraft to the job. Their arrival was carefully timed so that the convoy could capitalise on the confusion caused in the aftermath of the bombing raid. It was hoped that the enemy's attention would be diverted enough to help Campbeltown slip through the estuary under the noses of the defenders.

The bomber crews taking part were ordered only to drop their bombs onto targets they could see. Everyone was painfully aware of the proximity of the town to the port and the potential for civilian casualties which blind bombing would create.

Instead of the normal pattern of an RAF raid, where a single pass would be made over the target, the bombers began to circle over St. Nazaire. The cloud cover was such that only a few bombs were dropped, and these missed their targets....

The Germans were perplexed at the unusual air activity until someone suggested that the planes might be dropping paratroops. Paratroops over St. Nazaire, why? Of course, the docks! The British were dropping soldiers to attack the U-boat pens and the dry dock!

The call went out for all anti-aircraft batteries to extinguish their searchlights as the Germans suspected the RAF could be using them to home in on the area. A general alert was issued and all service personnel mobilised. In total, St. Nazaire was defended by 5,000 soldiers and sailors, including an entire infantry brigade. At the time Campbeltown was due to arrive it was hoped that most of them would be safely tucked up in bed. Now, unwittingly, the RAF made sure that every last one of the enemy was up and ready to defend the docks....

The now alert Germans began to look skywards, watching out for parachutists. However, not everyone had their eyes on the night sky, and an observant soldier stationed among the defences on the northern bank of the estuary reported that he had seen unusual activity out to sea. When this report made it back to the garrison commander at St. Nazaire, he ordered the coastal defences to stand to for a possible seaborne attack....

While this was happening, the flotilla suffered its first casualty. ML 341 developed a fault with her engines. There was absolutely no way repairs could be made so Commander Ryder ordered her withdrawal to the rendezvous point where she could meet the destroyers....

As the raiders approached the coastline they changed formation into the one they would use for the attack. While MGB 314 remained at the front of the flotilla, the MLs formed two line astern columns on Campbeltown's flanks....

At about this time the flotilla was spotted by a surfaced U-boat which had just left the estuary. Unseen by the British, the U-boat sent a hasty wireless signal to St. Nazaire saying that it had seen a British convoy moving westward. In actual fact the flotilla was steaming eastwards. How the U-boat crew made such a mistake will never be known, but their report served to further complicate matters for the commander at St. Nazaire. According to the sub, the British were moving away from St. Nazaire? These must be the same ships which had been spotted from the shore. Were they acting as a diversion for the parachute assault...?

***

At 0018, the flotilla reached the shallows at the mouth of the estuary. They were now being tracked by coastal radar, who supplied a report of the contact back to the garrison commander. The RAF were withdrawing and with them the threat of parachute landings. Reports from officers in and around the docks told the same story; all was quiet. However, the garrison commander remained uneasy. He decided to keep his men at the alert until he got to the bottom of the radar reports....

Campbeltown had picked up speed on the approach to the estuary and was now steaming at close to her maximum speed. In front of Campbeltown, in the command boat, the flotilla was being guided by the master navigator, Lieutenant Bill Green RN. It was Green's job to ensure the safe passage of Campbeltown through the endless shallows, mudflats and sandbanks which formed much of the estuary. His was not an enviable position, as even the slightest navigational error would see the Campbeltown stranded.

Also in MGB 314, Commander Ryder knew that the Germans would be watching the small force on their radar screens and that the coming moments would prove decisive....

As the flotilla came within range of the outer German defences, the beam from a searchlight suddenly stabbed through the darkness. It was looking for something, but aimed behind the British boats. For some inexplicable reason it went out as quickly as it came on, leaving the attack force free to steam deeper into the estuary....

The flotilla was suddenly through the first line of big guns without a shot being fired! All aboard wondered how long their luck would last. As they sailed towards the river, searchlights were playing across the water as the coastal batteries searched for the unknown ship. Several illuminating rounds were fired from the big guns, bursting high above the scene and bathing it in cold white light. Soon the Campbeltown was seen and immediately afterwards the whole flotilla was caught in the glare of a brace of searchlights from both banks of the estuary....

On the bridge of the Campbeltown, Lieutenant-Commander Beattie ordered his signaller to stand by with the Aldis lamp. He knew that at this speed, it would take his ship approximately eight minutes to reach the docks at St. Nazaire. If only they could buy themselves enough time....

As expected, a signal was seen from the northern bank. It was the challenge which everyone was expecting. The Germans were insisting that the ship immediately identify itself otherwise it would be fired upon. Just at that moment there was an almighty shudder which ran the length of the ship and threw everyone aboard off balance. They had hit the sandbank! This was no fault of Lieutenant Green, for he had expertly shown the way along the pre-plotted course. The fact was that the water wasn't quite as deep as even the twenty-four inches presumed! For a few awful seconds Campbeltown slowed then lurched but somehow kept going until she was clear....!

Beattie's signaller responded to the challenge with the correct Kriegsmarine codeword. The shore signal asked for confirmation and was given it in reply....

Aboard the command boat, Commander Ryder was visualising events at the enemy signals post. Lit up as they were, the Kriegsmarine flag was very much in evidence flying from the Campbeltown's mast. The Germans would be looking through ship recognition manuals in order to positively identify the mysterious vessel. She resembled a friendly warship, but from which class? She had responded correctly to the initial challenge, giving an answer known only to German ships. However, they hadn't been warned to expect the arrival of any Kriegsmarine ships that night. Meanwhile, those eight minutes were ticking away....

Everyone in the flotilla was on high alert. Some were watching the exchange of signals between the shore and Campbeltown, while the commandos crammed below decks in the MLs were listening for the first sounds of battle....

Another challenge was issued and responded to in the correct fashion by Campbeltown's signaller. Suddenly a warning burst of tracer was fired by a dual purpose anti-aircraft cannon from of one of the shore batteries. The tracer fire landed in front of the flotilla and prompted the Campbeltown to flash a signal – again in the current code – to tell those ashore to stop shooting. Another challenge was seen. The Germans repeated their demand to know who the flotilla was. Campbeltown replied that they were a friendly force who had sustained damage during an engagement with the enemy and were putting into St. Nazaire for the night.

Bewildered that they had no knowledge of the arrival of any Kriegsmarine unit, or just why the mysterious ship was sailing across the dangerous shallows, the shore batteries held their fire.

The Germans manning the shore defences had not been warned of the impending arrival of any Kriegsmarine ships, yet the small flotilla which was illuminated in the powerful beams of their searchlights had responded in the correct manner each and every time it was challenged. The British could not possibly know the current codewords and countersigns? Surely, they must be who they said they were...?

By now the Campbeltown was closing fast on the

mouth of the river. It had been five minutes since she had first been challenged. Five precious minutes which had allowed her to get within 2,000 yards of the dry dock. Thank god for good military intelligence...!

Without warning, the next burst of 20mm cannon fire was directed at the Campbeltown. She was hit but suffered little damage. Over in MGB 314, Commander Ryder grabbed for what he knew to be his star asset. The flare pistol was already loaded with the correct colour flare. For security reasons, the Germans made sure that the colour of the flares were changed on a daily basis. Thanks to Bletchley, The flotilla knew which was in use on that very night.

Ryder knew that firing the flare would immediately stop all incoming fire and allow his force to press on to the docks and that is why it was to be saved for the very last moment. He aimed skywards and fired. Instead of watching a brilliantly bright flare arc up into the night sky, the cartridge was a dud, falling out of the gun with a fizzle before tumbling into the sea....

By now the entire German defences had opened up. Knowing the game was up, Lieutenant-Commander Beattie ordered the Kriegsmarine flag be struck from Campbeltown's main mast and replaced by the White Ensign of the Royal Navy.

Upon Beattie's command, the Campbeltown's own guns began to reply to the enemy fire. .50 and 20mm calibre rounds poured into the shore defences. The noise was tremendous and the scene was lit by tracers flying over the water in both directions. Up near the bow, the quick firing 12 pounder gun was also in action, firing high explosive shells at the German emplacements....

Whatever the Campbeltown could deliver in terms of firepower, the enemy were able to respond in much greater strength. The old destroyer soon found herself bracketed by artillery, huge gouts of water erupting all about her as the high explosive shells tried to find their targets....

Now the little British flotilla found itself with more to contend with that the enemy shore defences. The Germans had a block ship anchored on the approach to the dock. The Sperrbrecher had been positioned carefully in order to arrest the approach on any naval attack force. She was armed with a variety of deck weapons including 88mm guns and dual purpose flak cannons and was able to bring fire down across the mouth of the Loire....

As the flotilla began to pass the Sperrbrecher, Able Seaman William 'Bill' Savage RN (who was aboard the Command MGB) opened up on the German ship with such accuracy that within a matter of seconds he had silenced its guns. The other MLs also fired upon the Sperrbrecher as they passed, ensuring that she remained out of action for the rest of the mission....

The incoming fire became exceptionally intense as the flotilla passed the block ship and the Campbeltown found herself being hit from all sides at close range.
 On the wheelhouse, the sailor steering the ship was killed. Another sailor stepped in to take his place and was also killed. Thinking that he was the only man left to steer, one of the commando officers; second in command of the demolition parties Captain Bob Montgomery, took control of the vessel. He had no idea of how to direct a large ship like Campbeltown, let alone get her into position where she would strike the target. Fortunately for all concerned, Lieutenant Tibbits – the Royal Navy officer responsible for designing the charges hidden in Campbeltown's forward section – was close at hand. Tapping Montgomery on the shoulder, an unruffled Tibbits said. "I'll take it, old boy." Getting behind the wheel and all but blinded by searchlights, Tibbits ignored

the incoming hail of fire and began his final preparations....

Down on the deck of the Campbeltown, the commandos were sheltering behind the armour plating running along the ships forward rails. The volume of fire now being directed at the Campbeltown was terrific, with 20, 37 and 40mm cannon shells striking her from bow to stern. The commandos were powerless to intervene in the fight; all they could do was endure the storm of lead bursting all about them....

Up on the wheelhouse, Tibbits was still struggling to see ahead. He was being directed by the equally cool under fire Beattie who had called for more speed for the final approach. The dazzling searchlights and tangle of tracer fire passing all around was conspiring to disorientate both men. Looking through his binoculars, Beattie finally began to make sense of the situation. He calculated that the Campbeltown was steaming further to port than planned and, fooled by the lighthouse at its mouth, was aiming towards the entrance to the Avant port. Just as he was about to call to Tibbits to correct the course, the German searchlights illuminated the lighthouse at the end of the the old mole, providing them with the perfect navigational aid. Pulling at the wheel, Tibbits brought the ship back onto the correct heading....

The MLs carrying the commando raiding teams had been cutting through the water at speed. They were all under very heavy fire and a couple had already been hit. Large calibre tracer rounds were flying dangerously overhead and all around, skipping off the water and causing the surface of the river to bubble and boil as the Germans attempted to home in on the fast moving vessels.
Everyone was mindful of the exposed long range petrol tanks up on the decks of the flimsy craft. One cannon or

bullet strike, even a hot shard of shrapnel would see them ruptured and the unfortunate boat immediately engulfed in flames....

Still at the ships wheel, Lieutenant Tibbits followed Lieutenant Commander Beattie's instructions and steered Campbeltown past the old mole. Despite the fire emanating from it and the neighbouring piers, fire which was striking the wheelhouse and zipping inches from their heads, both officers remained icily calm. Indeed, one witness to the scene later described Beattie as 'positively Elizabethan' in his attitude towards danger.

The clang and crash of cannon and machinegun fire raking the ship fused with the sound of battle to create one long cacophony of noise above which it was all but impossible to be heard, yet Beattie kept up his stream of commands to which Tibbits instantly responded.

There, appearing away to port from behind the old mole was their target! Campbeltown was now steaming at full speed. In anticipation of what was to come next, the crew of the 12 pounder began to retire sternwards as fast as they were able....

Every enemy searchlight and gun was trained on the ship as she careered towards the dry dock gates. She tore through the torpedo nets strung across the approach which protected the gates from an aerial torpedo attack. Her own guns blazing and the White Ensign flying defiantly, Campbeltown's bow was heading straight for the very centre of the target....

Suddenly there was an almighty crash. The render of twisted metal was so loud that it momentarily drowned out the noise of battle. Such was the force of the impact that the whole of the bow was buckled some thirty-six feet back and the ship rode up so she was perched precariously on top of the gates. Just as Tibbits had calculated, the explosive charges were now pressed against them....

The time was 0134. Amazingly, the Campbeltown was only four minutes off the moment she was scheduled to hit the gates....

Although they had braced themselves for impact, the men aboard Campbeltown were thrown into disarray by its ferocity. Now the commandos had to move, and move fast. The ship was still in the glare of searchlights and being subjected to extremely heavy fire from both sides. It was into this maelstrom that the commandos had to plunge themselves....

MTB 74 had been following the Campbeltown; ready to fire her torpedoes at the dry dock gates should the ship fail to hit it. Sub-Lieutenant Wynn watched in amazement as the Campbeltown careered into the target in defiance of every enemy effort to stop her. Satisfied that there was now no need for him to attack, he immediately ordered the sailor at the wheel of his boat to cut away toward the secondary target. There he would loiter until he received confirmation from Commander Ryder that Campbeltown was indeed where she needed to be and permission for his torpedoes to be fired into the old lock gates....

The protection parties were the first to leave Campbeltown, deploying rapidly to their designated points whilst under heavy fire from machinegun emplacements dotted about the vicinity. Once there they set about trying to suppress the German fire and clear a path for the demolition teams who themselves were now scrambling from the ship....

Lieutenant John Roderick and his team were one of the first off the ship. With breathtaking professionalism they stormed the nearby enemy positions to clear a path for the demolitions teams. A pair of machinegun emplacements was quickly dealt with using grenades before Roderick and his men moved on to destroy an anti-aircraft gun....

At the same time, Captain Donald Roy was leading his group of Scots commandos out across the quayside. Roy's party were all dressed in kilts and must have presented a fearsome sight to the Germans. Passing the pump house, they quickly silenced the guns on its flat roof with a concentration of accurate fire.

Onwards the Scotsmen battled, fighting their way through the enemy opposition and out across the nearby bridge which separated the Bassin's St. Nazaire and Penhoet. There they 'went firm', taking up defensive positions in order to stop any counter-attack and interference with the demolitions parties.

The Scots were subjected to murderous fire from several points, including boats moored nearby and a 40mm anti-aircraft gun emplacement. Soon the commandos began to take casualties.

Determined to defend the bridge at all costs, although severely outnumbered and outgunned, Roy's men gave as good as they got. In fact, the captain of one of the harbour defence boats which was engaged in the action became so convinced that the Scotsmen were going to capture his vessel that he scuttled her....

Major Copland was the last soldier to leave Campbeltown. He made a quick sweep of the deck to make sure no one had been left aboard the Campbeltown by mistake. The wounded were to be removed to as safe a place as possible until they could be taken onto the MLs. At this point, Copland was unsure if the severity of the impact had somehow interfered with the delayed action fuse. The amatol might just explode at any time....

Below deck, the Campbeltown's sea cocks were opened. If, for any reason, the charges failed to detonate, by scuttling her, the enemy operation to remove the ship would be made that much more difficult....

Meanwhile, the second landing party were making their own approach to the slipway by the old mole. They were under intense fire all the way in and several of the MLs were hit and seriously damaged. The sailors manning the guns on the MLs replied in kind, doing their best to suppress the enemy, but their best efforts had little effect against an enemy fighting from fortified positions....

Although he had no need to, Lieutenant-Colonel Newman went in with his troops, MGB 314 putting him and his seven man HQ team ashore. Almost at once, this small team found themselves in the centre of a furious gun battle. They were being fired at by one of the machineguns on the old mole, from several positions on top of the U-boat pens and a few of the enemy boats moored nearby....

Given the sheer volume of fire, of the six MLs scheduled, only two others managed to land their full complement of commandos. One made it to the mole after MGB 314 while the other put the troops ashore in the old entrance....

Sergeant Major Haines was in command of the party which suddenly found itself under fire at the old entrance. Detached from the other teams, Haines immediately made radio contact with Lieutenant-Colonel Newman. The Colonel advised the Sergeant Major to make their way to the HQ team with all speed, as his detachment of fourteen were now the only available reserve....

Out on the water the enemy continued to concentrate their fire on the MLs. Commando officer Captain Mickey Burn's group was aboard one of those attempting to reach the old mole. The boat received a direct hit which set it on fire. Ablaze and out of control, the boat drifted helplessly on the tide. Captain Burn found himself in the water as he made to escape the blazing ML and was pulled ashore by one of his Corporals. He was the only man amongst his team to make it to land unwounded....

With the bulk of the men assigned to attack the old mole, anti-aircraft emplacements, power station and other targets unable to land. Colonel Newman faced a new dilemma. He simply didn't have enough troops to carry out the taskings. The Concrete anti-aircraft emplacement sited halfway along the mole could not be taken. The German machinegunners stationed within had a clear field of fire along its length and across all approaches. They were laying down murderous fire against anything or anyone who appeared within range.
The Colonel ordered his small force to set up a perimeter around the base of the old mole and ready themselves to fight off the inevitable counter-attack....

Meanwhile, over at the Normandie dock, defended all the way from the Campbeltown by the protection teams, the demolitions squads soon found themselves at their respective targets....

Lieutenant Stuart Chant and his men had been given the job of destroying the machinery inside the pump house which was responsible for emptying the dry dock. While they made it to their objective without incurring any losses, they had all been wounded while aboard Campbeltown.
Trying the door to the pump house, Chant found it locked. In all of the planning and preparation for the operation, everyone had overlooked the fact that the door might not be open! It was a sturdy steel door, set into a larger pair and so could not simply be kicked in. Chant's own explosives were unsuitable for the task of blowing the door open, so a few minutes were wasted while a small charge was fashioned from spare plastic explosive.

The charge did its job and the commandos were inside. They found themselves on the ground floor of the pump house. Fortunately, they encountered no resistance or civilian workers inside so set about deploying with all speed....

The four huge pumps were located some forty feet below and could only be accessed via seven flights of narrow iron stairs. Chant and four of his men searched through the darkness until they found the head of the stairway and began a rapid descent....

Lieutenant Chant had been hit in the hand, neck and both legs and was painfully aware that once the charges were set, he and his men would have only a short window of opportunity to escape the explosions. Navigating the latticework of walkways and steps in the pitch blackness would be a tough enough challenge for any commando, but for wounded men it would be nigh impossible. Knowing that he had no chance of making it out, Chant had ordered the most severely wounded man to stay behind to guard the top of the stairs. His rucksack containing the specially made demolition charges was taken and carried by the others....

Halfway down the third flight of stairs, Chant encountered his second problem. In the darkness he could see that the walkways were nothing like the ones he had encountered in training. They were a confusing 'spaghetti jungle' of metal walkways, half of which appeared to lead to nothing but dead ends. Knowing that they had but a matter of seconds to clear the building before the charges detonated, it would be all too easy for his team to become disorientated as they attempted to scramble back up the ground floor....

With each man following the other by holding on to the man in front's rucksack, Chant led his team down into the dark bowels of the building. The further they descended the more the terrific sound of the battle raging across the docks subsided until it was overtaken by the clattering of their boots on the iron steps to the accompaniment of one of the team who was whistling 'The White Cliffs of Dover'....

Once among the pumps, the commandos were relieved to find that they were of the same design as the ones they had practised on. The men rifled through their rucksacks and produced the specially prepared explosive charges then set about placing them, eight per pump, on top of the pumps at exactly the point where they would render the most damage. No-one had to be told what do; they knew where to lay the explosives and their training had conditioned them to be able to operate in the near pitch blackness.

The charges themselves each weighed five pounds. They were all waterproofed and had duplicate leads. Combined, the shattering effect of the explosives was enough to completely wreck the machinery. The commandos knew that pumps of this type would be virtually impossible to replace and were told that as a result of their action, the pump house would be out of commission for at least one year....

After the charges were laid, Chant and his men set about the task of connecting them to a 'ring main' of detonation cord. Once complete, Chant inspected the whole of the demolition package in order to satisfy himself everything was where it should be and connected properly. Once he ignited the short section of slow burning fuse the commandos would have just ninety seconds to get out of the building before the powerful plastic explosives ripped through it. He sent all but one of his men up to remove their colleague at the top of the stairs and when he was sure they were clear, he pulled the percussion cap exploder. The fuse began to sizzle and Chant knew it was time to go. He had asked this one man to stay with him because he was doubtful that his wounds would allow him to get up the stairs without assistance before the explosives detonated....

Chant and the remaining man attacked the stairs, running like hell as fast as their wounds would allow. Miraculously they made it out onto the ground floor then through the door with a few seconds to spare....

Crouching beside the building for shelter from the blast and incoming enemy fire, Chant and his men waited. Sensing that they were a little too close for comfort, Captain Montgomery waved them away. No sooner had they cleared the scene the charges went off.

Such was the violence of the explosions that all the masonry from the roof came crashing down right on top of the point where Chant's team had taken cover...!

Inside the pump house the destruction was total. Not only had the pumps themselves been destroyed but much of the interior of the building had caved in on itself, piling tons of steel and concrete upon the shattered machinery....

With Campbeltown wedged firmly into the southern gates of the Normandie dry dock, the commandos wanted to ensure the gates at the other end also received their attention....

Under heavy fire, Lieutenant Robert 'Bob' Burtenshaw led his men along the edge of the dry dock to the northern gates. Burtenshaw had somehow taken possession of Lieutenant-Commander Beattie's peaked hat and was wearing it all the way to the target while singing 'They'll Always Be An England' at the top of his voice.

Whilst moving forward, Burtenshaw happened upon another small team of commandos. These men were those left of Lieutenant Gerard Brett's party. Brett's team had been caught in terrific crossfire as they moved away from Campbeltown. Brett and many of his men were wounded and unable to continue so Brett ordered the rest to continue on towards the northern dock gates....

By this time Burtenshaw and several of his own men had been wounded. Leading this combined force while still under fire, he ran forwards until he and his men reached their objective.

Burtenshaw then set about organising his small force. Together, they began to lower twelve 18-pound demolition charges into the water. The demolition charges rested against the face of the gates. As with the famous 'Dambusters' bouncing bombs, science dictated that – just as long as they were in contact with the target, the energy created by the explosions would be directed forwards into the gates, blowing holes into them in a dozen places. Even the relatively small charges would cause damage disproportionate to their size, which the enemy would find difficult and time consuming to repair....

While they worked the enemy were raking Burtenshaw's party with automatic fire. Much of the shooting emanated from some of the boats moored in the Bassin de St. Nazaire. Burtenshaw decided he had had enough of the Germans, so got a small team together to go and suppress their fire. Although he and most of his men were only armed with pistols, they charged at the enemy guns, shooting all the way. Burtenshaw was still singing 'They'll Always Be An England'. He was hit and fell dead at the dockside, but not before he had seen the enemy begin to break and run....

Their job complete and fuses lit, the commandos began to withdraw from the dry dock gates....

***

Although they were responding in strength, the German defenders were confused. It appeared they were being attacked from all points by a large British landing force. When the garrison commander received a telephone call to inform him of the attack, he didn't believe the caller, in fact he thought he was drunk and put him on a charge. It wasn't until he was informed that the information had come directly from the port commander at St. Nazaire that he took the call seriously.

The garrison commander hurried on foot to the nearby U-boat pens. He arrived to find troops deployed to defend the pens against imminent attack, while the submarines inside were being rigged for scuttling to stop them from falling into British hands. The commander ordered that all approaches to the pens were sealed off. Soon German troops were rushing to deploy at the bridges....

It was thirty minutes since Campbeltown hit the dock gates. The commandos had made the most of their time ashore. Aside from the pump house, the winding gear at both ends of the Normandie dock had been destroyed by other demolitions teams. All enemy anti-aircraft emplacements around the main target were overrun and their guns spiked, while inroads into the adjacent underground fuel storage depot had been made....

South of the Normandie dry dock, Colonel Newman's small force of men could do little except consolidate their defences. Given their small number and the ferocity of the German response, there was no hope of this particular commandos fighting through to their objectives....

About 300 yards south of the old mole, where his band of wounded stragglers had made it to shore from their wrecked ML, there seemed little hope for Captain Burn. His men were scattered and those he saw appeared to have lost their weapons and demolitions kit during their escape from the burning ML. Indeed Captain Burn's own Thompson had gone to the bottom of the river. Now all he had was his pistol and a few grenades. The scale of their wounds meant that, as a fighting unit, those around Burn had effectively ceased to exist. He instructed the men to make their way along the dockside as best as they were able until they met up with Colonel Newman's Party where they would be embarked on the MLs then removed from the scene....

Undaunted and alone, Captain Burn began to advance on the target he had been designated to attack. His targets lay some distance from him and Burn was under the impression that the two anti-aircraft gun towers had been shooting at the flotilla ever since it had gotten within range. He also knew the twin barrelled 37mm guns posed a great danger to the MLs as they left the scene, so it was imperative they were put out of action....

Burn dodged from cover to cover as he made his way towards his objective. He found the area to be fairly quiet and certainly devoid of the furious action which was happening at other points.

Suddenly he heard German voices close by. Burn grabbed for a grenade and pulled the pin. His intention was to lob it in amongst the voices and hopefully kill or wound as many as possible. Realising that his best course of action was to continue without being seen, he changed his mind and moved off into the shadows. It was a tense few minutes for Burn as he dodged enemy patrols to get within striking distance of the gun towers. He suddenly remembered that he was still holding onto the grenade so threw it into the water where it exploded harmlessly....

Finally arriving at the target, Burn realised that both

towers were not in action. He had no explosives and only his handgun but he knew that as a matter of course, if they were physically able, the remnants of his team who had landed elsewhere would immediately strike out for the gun towers. Burn hoped to link up with them and lead the attack. He waited but no one came. Finally acknowledging that they wouldn't arrive, he crept forward and attempted to set fire to the towers with the only things in his possession which could do the job. Both towers were partly constructed from wood, so Burn threw his only two incendiary grenades into them in the hope it would be enough to render them useless. It was an impossible gamble, but it worked, soon the wooden elements of the towers were alight. Burn knew that the enemy would now be unable to bring the guns into action. Slowly, and mindful of the fact that German soldiers were all around, he retraced his steps back into the shadows….

Meanwhile, the commandos were oblivious to the disaster overtaking the MLs. Those carrying troops who hadn't been able to land had already been instructed to withdraw to the open ocean, leaving just a few boats available to rescue the shore parties. Even the couple of boats which were acting as reserves in case other MLs were sunk were themselves put out of action. Some became disorientated in the confusion of battle while others were hit and set ablaze as they stood by to embark Lieutenant-Colonel Newman's men….

***

Ignoring the hail of fire which was raining down all around her, MGB 314 came into the old entrance. Commander Ryder stepped ashore then made for Campbeltown to verify that she had been scuttled and the delayed action fuse initiated. While he was away some of the wounded were embarked upon the MGB.

Satisfied that Campbeltown was well and truly wedged into the dry dock gates and her deadly payload on its countdown to explode, Ryder ordered Sub-Lieutenant Wynn in MTB 74 to fire her torpedoes into the gates at the entrance to the Bassin de Dt. Nazaire. MTB 74 was quickly brought into position then released her two torpedoes. Wynn actually heard the thud as they struck the gates before sinking to the bottom. In two hours time they would explode, wrecking the gates....

As soon as MTB 74 had done her job, Commander Ryder ordered her to leave the area and steam to the rendezvous point where the Atherton and Tyneside were waiting to escort the flotilla home. With the throttles open, MTB 74 sped away from the scene at 40 knots.

She was harried all the way by enemy fire and several times came within a hairs breath of being hit....

Once out into the estuary, Wynn suddenly spotted some survivors clinging to a piece of floating wreckage. Up to this point, the only thing which had allowed MTB 74 to successfully run the gauntlet of German fire was her speed. If he stopped, Wynn knew would be endangering his boat. She would be quickly bracketed by fire and almost certainly hit. Wynn knew it would take only one round in the petrol tanks to set his boat ablaze. However, if he carried on past the stranded men there was every chance they would be swept out to sea and drowned.

Wynn ordered the boat to a halt and take aboard the survivors. Almost as soon as she came to a standstill, MTB 74 was hit by a German shell. Wynn was knocked unconscious then blown overboard. His eye was taken out by the blast. When he came to, he saw his boat engulfed in flames and its two deck mounted petrol tanks leaking burning fuel into the sea. Wynn had been pulled onto a life raft by one of his crewmen and his life was saved as a result. Terribly injured, Wynn could do nothing except look on as MTB 74 went through her death throws....

As she withdrew, ML 177 was attempting to make her way through the storm of enemy fire now being brought down across the whole of the estuary ....

Shorty beforehand, having been subjected to much incoming fire, ML 177 had gone into the area of the Normandie dry dock with the express intention of landing Sergeant Major Haines party. She was the only boat to have successfully deposited troops in the old entrance.

Before long her task had become that of evacuating as many men as possible and to this end, while still under fire, had come alongside Campbeltown....

Crammed onto the deck of ML 177 as she made her way across the estuary was Lieutenant Tibbits, half of the Campbeltown's crew and some of the wounded commandos. The ML powered through the water at top speed, harried all the way by tracers from the anti-aircraft batteries and high explosive shells fired by coastal artillery.

Suddenly ML 177 took a direct hit. Her captain, Lieutenant Mark Rodier RNVR, was killed along with Tibbits and several other men. The vessel was set alight amidships and such was the ferocity of the flames that it appeared the boat would be quickly engulfed.

Lieutenant-Commander Beattie, the officer commanding HMS Campbeltown, was also aboard the boat and organised the men to fight the flames in the hope of regaining control then sailing on to the open sea and the rendezvous with the waiting destroyers. Once – if – they arrived, Beattie knew the survivors would be safe....

After fighting the fire for ten minutes or so while still being shot at, Beattie realised the position was hopeless. ML 177 could not be saved. He gave the order to abandon ship. He jumped into the cold waters of the estuary and began to swim away....

Lieutenant Tom Boyd RNVR was in command of ML 160. His boat had been in the thick of the action ever since the Germans realised they were under attack. As well as providing supporting fire to the commandos, his crew managed to knock out an enemy coastal gun.

He too was withdrawing from St. Nazaire until he came across another ML which had been hit and disabled.

ML 447 was carrying the only commando party equipped to clear the old mole of its pillboxes. She had come in to the mole but was subjected to heavy machinegun fire and grenade attacks from the Germans as she attempted to land the assault team. Most of the commandos and ML 447s crew were wounded and she was set on fire in the encounter. The battered ML had no option to withdraw out into the river where the flames could be fought.

After receiving the order to withdraw, ML 447 was attempting to run the gauntlet of fire through the estuary when she was hit and immobilised.

Boyd saw that the mortally damaged boat was still under very heavy fire and those aboard had no way of escape. If the petrol tanks were hit then ML 447 and all those on her would be blown to kingdom come.

Drawing up alongside, ML 160 was able to bring aboard everyone from the stricken boat before powering away under a barrage of German fire....

The loss of this particular commando assault team led by Captain David Birney, who was aboard ML 447, was to have disastrous consequences for the shore parties....

ML 267 was carrying another party of commandos led by Regimental Sergeant Major Moss. In the confusion of the close quarters fighting, she ran too far up river. Realising the mistake her Captain, Lieutenant Eric Beart

RNVR turned the ML about and made his way back towards the Normandie dock. Passing a dredger, the commandos attacked it with grenades.

ML 267 came in at the stern of HMS Campbeltown then attempted to enter the old entrance. The ML was subjected to intense fire all the way but managed to reach a point where she could disembark the troops. Only a few commandos made it ashore but they were soon forced back to the boat by the sheer volume of enemy fire. ML 447 had nowhere to go except to reverse into the river. She was raked with cannon rounds and set on fire. Some of the commandos, including RSM Moss, were killed and the boat abandoned….

For ML 268 the story was even more tragic. During the final run in by HMS Campbeltown towards the Normandie dry dock gates, 268 was manoeuvring to bring her complement of commandos ashore at the old entrance.

Aboard, along with the crew, were one of the five-man strong demolition teams and its protection party and a detachment from RSM Moss' team.

After being landed, the demolition team, led by Captain Harry Pennington, was to move forward to the northernmost bridge which connected the area around the Normandie dock to the rest of the port. After the bridge had been secured by Lieutenant Morgan Jenkins' accompanying protection party, Pennington's men were to destroy it with explosives. Once out of action, the commando's northern area of operations would be secured against counter attack….

As ML 268 made her approach she received a direct hit from one of the anti-aircraft guns mounted on top of the U-boat pens. The round – possibly an explosive tipped one – probably hit the MLs inboard fuel tanks. ML 268 exploded. Of the sailors and commandos aboard, only two survived….

The bridge, which was vital to the commando's safety, remained intact and open to the enemy....

***

By this time the commandos around the Normandie dock had completed all their primary objectives. It was now time to retreat to the old mole where they hoped to embark and be taken to safety....

At Lieutenant-Colonel Newman's shore HQ, the failure to destroy the emplacements on the old mole were beginning to tell. Still, and hoping that the boats could suppress the enemy sufficiently enough to allow them to come alongside the slipway; preparations were being made for the commandos to retire to the old mole where they could be re-embarked and removed....

However, it appeared that the Germans wouldn't let them get away so easily. Aside from incessant shooting from the positions on the mole itself, extremely heavy fire from machineguns and dual purpose anti-aircraft cannons sited on top of the nearby U-boat pens was now being concentrated on and around Newman's position. He knew that he men would be forced to run the gauntlet of this fire as they made their way to the old mole. Asking Sergeant Major Haines if he had anything to counter the enemy, he was told that Haines had a two inch mortar. The Colonel instructed Haines to attend to the matter with all speed....

Quickly, the Sergeant Major had the mortar set up. Somehow the sight had gone missing so it ranged on the U-boat pens by eye. The supply of high explosive rounds was plentiful so, and needing little adjustment, the mortar crew began to rain them down onto the top of the pens. The roof of the U-boat pens was a flat expanse of bomb proof concrete so, as a result, when each mortar round burst it did so on the very surface of the roof, sending shrapnel away in all directions. Soon – and with supporting fire from a couple of Bren guns – the mortar crew had silenced some of the guns by direct hits and driven the crews away from others, markedly decreasing the volume of enemy fire....

Captain Mickey Burn was still cut off from the main HQ group. As he made his way to the safety of the commando's lines at the old mole area, he suddenly found himself confronted by three German soldiers. The Germans appeared unsure of what to do with the Britisher and began to debate amongst themselves if they should shoot him. Burn spoke German and followed the conversation with growing trepidation. Quickly, speaking in German, Burn announced that it would be foolish for the men to execute him as he was an officer and, as such, would make an important prisoner.

Burn continued to talk to the Germans, all the while walking backwards towards where he thought Colonel Newman's HQ was. Foolishly, and without taking control of their prisoner, they followed on.

Abruptly, out of the darkness came a challenge. It was Sergeant Major Haines. The three Germans were so shocked to find themselves in such close proximity to the British that they simply turned and ran away. Burn shouted a reply to Haines and was quickly waved to safety....

Out on the water, ten of the flimsy MLs had been destroyed. They were floating wrecks, most on fire and abandoned. Recognising that it presented a serious and immediate threat, the pillbox on the old mole had itself been temporarily silenced by MGB 314s gunner. Able Seaman Savage had proved his worth when he knocked out the guns on the Sperrbrecher. Having turned his attention to the old mole, Savage's shooting was no less deadly. Had it not been for his actions, more boats and commandos would have fallen victim to the pillbox. Sadly, Able Seaman Savage would not survive the night....

Because of the fact that the demolition team designated to destroy it had been killed before they could get ashore, the vital crossing into the area around the Normandie dock was now being used by the Germans. They were pouring troops across it in preparation for a counter attack. Because the commandos were falling back in readiness for the extraction phase, the enemy found their progress to be largely unhindered. The Germans soon found themselves taking up positions at the water's edge in and around the Normandie dry dock and the old entrance....

Out on the river, once it became apparent that, by virtue fact that the only two places where it was possible to take them off were firmly in enemy hands, the commandos could not be embarked, Commander Ryder knew he had no alternative but to give the order to withdraw.

The few boats surviving, who had so valiantly ridden the storm of enemy fire as they waited to lift off the shore parties, now turned towards the estuary. All aboard were sickened by the fact that they appeared to be abandoning the commandos. They knew there weren't enough MLs left afloat to evacuate but a fraction of those still fighting but the crews were still willing to run the gauntlet of German fire in order to rescue as many as they could....

Captain Bob Montgomery had picked his way through the firefights which were happening all around him and made it to Lieutenant-Colonel Newman. He reported that all the primary targets had been demolished. The equipment in the pump house and both winding gear houses which serviced the giant Normandie dock were now destroyed beyond repair. He also believed that the northern gates at the Normandie dry dock had been damaged by Lieutenant Burtenshaw's team. Montgomery then asked if he could be deployed elsewhere to help destroy any other targets before withdrawing by ML from the old mole. At that point, another officer drew Montgomery's attention to the mole and then the river. He was shocked to see the enemy still in control of the old mole. The sight of MLs on fire and out of action quickly made Montgomery realise there would be no escape by water....

The whole scene was now backlit by the glow of burning boats, petrol on the water and punctuated by tracer rounds and incessant muzzle flashes from countless guns. The Germans had recovered from their initial shock and were now closing in for the kill. The British were outnumbered more than ten to one but they had one mighty advantage; they were commandos....

Lieutenant-Colonel Newman, his second in command Major Bill Copland and another officer had a hurried conference.

With no way out across the water, Newman and his team had to decide upon another course of action. Whatever plan B was, they knew they would have to put it into operation with all speed....

It was during this conference that an enterprising German soldier managed to penetrate the commando lines. The man in question must have realised he had stumbled upon the British HQ. Pulling out a stick grenade, he lobbed it into the target. The grenade landed amongst Newman and his two officers then exploded. Amazingly, no one was hurt...!

Assessing the situation, things didn't look good for the commandos. After completing their various taskings, they had withdrawn in readiness for the extraction phase. The Germans moved quickly to occupy the ground on their side of the bridges which led inland from the Normandie dock and Bassin de St. Nazaire areas, effectively sealing the commandos off. This, of course, would not have been an issue had the old mole been taken. But now, with their escape route gone, the British had no alternative but to break out into the town if they wanted to escape the encirclement....

There could be no finesse about the plan to remove the commandos from the port. Hastily, they were ordered to report to a reorganisation area where they would have a brief opportunity to sort themselves out before making their move. Colonel Newman's instruction was simple; the commandos were to fight their way out of the docks and into the town. From there they should endeavour to scatter into the countryside then make their way south to neutral Spain....

As a military plan, the scheme was terribly flawed but the commandos had but two choices; fight or surrender. Not one man, be he wounded or not, was willing to lay down his arms. Therefore an all out assault against the most viable route out of the port was put into effect....

Colonel Newman had decided that the least worst of the breakout scenarios was a full frontal assault across the swing bridge which spanned the gap across the new lock next to the Bassin de St. Nazaire. Once across, the Colonel thought his men would have the best chance of fanning out into the town and beyond....

Moving out from the reorganisation point, the commandos wound their way through the maze of buildings, railway sidings and narrow streets which bisected the whole of that part of the port, bumping into small groups of enemy soldiers all the way. Finding themselves in a seemingly never ending series of vicious close quarter's firefights, the commandos began to do what they did best. Utterly fearless, they charged at the enemy and fought through their positions, killing or driving them off to clear their way ahead....

Lieutenant Stuart Chant (the officer who had led the attack on the pump house) was wounded again in one of these encounters. A couple of his men picked him up and carried him for some way until Chant told them to leave him behind. He knew that their ability to successfully break through the enemy cordon would be seriously compromised if they were carrying a wounded man. The men protested but Chant was adamant. He watched them disappear into the darkness towards the sound of yet another gun battle.

Chant suddenly realised he was danger close to the Campbeltown. He had no idea when the explosives contained in her bow were due to go off but knew he didn't want to be there when they did.

Suddenly, from out of nowhere appeared a young commando. He had become detached from the main body and was obviously disorientated. He sat down beside Chant. Chant suspected the man had been caught too near an explosion as he appeared a little dazed. It was obvious that the soldier had little chance of catching up with the rest of the commandos, so Chant instructed him to go off in search of a small boat in which they could make their own escape.

Eventually the young private returned. He had not been able to locate a boat. He lay down next to Chant as the Lieutenant attempted to work out their next move.

Before long, two Germans appeared. They shouted at Chant and the soldier to stand up. The young private complied and was immediately shot dead at point blank range. They then called for Chant to get to his feet.

Chant's wounds meant he was unable to move. Pointing their sub-machineguns, the Germans closed to stand either side of him. Suddenly, one of them said "Offizier?!" He had seen Chant's shoulder pips. Chant nodded in reply. They picked him up then carried him to a point where he was taken into the custody of other troops. Thankfully for the tight lipped Chant, it was further away from the Campbeltown that his previous position....

The rest of the commandos had now fought their way through to the swing bridge. The enemy attempted to check their progress almost every step of the way but their discipline, training and sheer aggression meant the British had made it to within spitting distance of a breakout. There was no time to stop and collect thoughts. Campbeltown was due to explode and they had to be as far away as possible before the four and a half tons of high explosives went up....

The Germans had not been idle. After the initial confusion they quickly moved to cut off the British from the expected attack on the U-boat pens. All the bridges had been fortified with heavily armed troops who were determined not to let the commandos pass.

The swing bridge was of the truss type. A metal construction, it was a latticework of girders with a roadway just wide enough to allow two way traffic to cross. The Germans had taken up position on the western end and the commandos knew they would have to run the gauntlet straight into the teeth of the enemy if they were to get to the other side....

For their part, the Germans knew that there could be no possibility of anyone crossing the bridge, let alone making it to the other side without being mown down by the sheer weight of fire they were now able to bring to bear. It would be an act of suicidal insanity for the British to do anything but surrender....

Without further ado, and with Lieutenant-Colonel Newman leading the way, the commandos charged onto the bridge, their guns blazing. Almost immediately the Germans replied with a fusillade of rifle and machinegun fire. They were joined by anti-aircraft guns sited nearby. It seemed every weapon the Germans had was now being pointed at the swing bridge. A tremendous amount of tracer was coming from three directions to converge on the bridge, clanging into the girders and the metal roadway before ricocheting away in wild tangents. The commandos began to take casualties, but the seemingly suicidal charge paid off. Much to the astonishment of everyone involved, they made it across the bridge and through the enemy lines, shooting their Thompsons', Bren's and captured weapons all the way….

Before long they had splintered into small groups in order to make it more difficult for the Germans to follow them up. They entered St. Nazaire town and began picking their way along side streets, across back gardens, over fences and through buildings. By now the commandos were thoroughly exhausted. Carrying their wounded, most of the groups realised the need to lay up and rest and tend to the injured men….

***

By dawn, Ryder's MGB 314 and four MLs managed to link up with the destroyers. Atherton and Tyneside had been joined by HMS Brocklesby and HMS Cleveland. In the early morning light it became obvious that all the small boats had suffered grievously during the operation and were badly shot up. They were packed with wounded and their decks slippery with blood. With no time to lose, the injured men were taken aboard the destroyers for treatment. The rest of the raiders abandoned the battered boats and looked on forlornly as they were scuttled. Ryder was sure no one else had made it out of the estuary so the order was given to set sail for England....

Little did Commander Ryder know, but three other MLs had successfully managed to power their way through the German shore defences. Under heavy fire all the way from the mouth of the river, they finally broke contact, speeding out of the estuary to safety. One of them was ML 160, the boat who had stopped in the face of a stream of cannon and artillery fire to take aboard men from a stricken launch....

After abandoning the burning boat which was attempting to take him and half of the Campbeltown's crew to safety, Lieutenant-Commander Beattie had swum to a 'Carley Float' life boat. It was full of other survivors so he was forced to hang on the side. He clung onto the raft until the next morning, when he and the rest of the men were picked up by a German patrol vessel....

***

During the hours of darkness the running firefight between the commandos and the troops of the German garrison lasted until the British ran out of ammunition....

Some of the commandos found themselves cornered and unable to fight back, they could do nothing except surrender. For others who had managed to escape the attentions of the hundreds of enemy troops now flooding St. Nazaire town, the story was different. Finding places to hide was not the easiest of tasks. The enemy was actively searching for them, going from house to house and garden to garden. When it got light the Germans would really begin to concentrate their search efforts and would leave little scope for successful evasion....

By around 1000hrs the following morning an eerie calm had settled across the docks. Only a few hours earlier the whole place was alive with the tremendous noise of battle. Now, in its place was relative quiet, but one look from any vantage point was all it took to see the devastation wrought by the British. Over in the Normandie dry dock, the battered hulk of HMS Campbeltown was perched precariously where she had imbedded herself into the dock gates. Her stern had settled to the bottom of the water and the Germans who knew about such things could see she had been scuttled in an attempt to make her removal more difficult....

Elsewhere across the docks, smoke still drifted in the breeze from the fires caused by some of the explosions and it caught in the throats of those inspecting the damage. Rolling stock and locomotives which the British found in the vicinity had been attacked with explosives and put out of action and sections the tracks themselves destroyed. Many of the defence structures and emplacements were knocked out and the guns within rendered useless. At the Normandie dock itself, the pump house and winding houses which serviced the dry dock were wrecked and the northern dock gates damaged. Yes, the British had caused much damage, some of it incredibly serious, but the Germans were in agreement that they had failed in their main objective; to destroy the dock gates. How the Royal Navy ever hoped to smash through the Normandie dock entrance with a small destroyer was beyond comprehension....

German officers and troops began to board HMS Campbeltown. Most were simply curious, some were seeking souvenirs, but others conducted a search just to make sure the British had not left any surprises behind....

Some hours had passed since the explosives aboard Campbeltown were timed to detonate. Perhaps, after the shock of hitting the gates, the fuses had somehow become detached?

Over at the old dock gates, the two torpedoes fired by MTB 74 had also failed to explode. They should have gone off at roughly the same time as the Campbeltown's charges....

The Germans had been busy bringing in survivors from the sunken MLs, many of whom had spent the night clinging to wreckage in the cold water....

One of the MLs – 306 – had found it impossible to land its complement of commandos during the attack. The ML waited in the hope of an opportunity to get to the dockside presenting itself but no such chance arose. So, still fully loaded with men, the boat had withdrawn after receiving the order from Ryder....

ML 306 managed to slip the net of ferocious enemy fire and break out into the open ocean. Making her way home alone, she was attacked by a Kriegsmarine destroyer The Jaguar. The expected course of action would have been for the ML to simply submit, but both her crew, and especially the commandos, were angry at not having the opportunity to get to grips with the enemy at the docks so they decided to take the ship on and hopefully make good an escape in the process....

A brief but furious firefight ensued, with the ML firing its cannon and machineguns and the commandos shooting their own weapons. It was a one sided affair, the little wooden ML stood no chance against the heavily armed warship yet, for a brief period, she raked the destroyer with small arms and Oerlikon fire. The shooting had little effect on the armour plated German vessel. Because they were so close; only fifty yards from each other, the destroyer was unable to bring its main armament to bear on the ML, however it could shoot back with Anti-aircraft and machineguns....

ML 306's Captain, Lieutenant Ian Henderson, was killed. One of the commandos, Sergeant Thomas Frank Durrant had been manning a stern mounted twin Vickers machinegun for most of the mission. During both the attack and withdrawal, Durrant had kept up steady stream of fire on enemy emplacements. Despite being wounded he refused to leave his position. In the action against The Jaguar, he was exposed to enemy fire and hit and wounded another twelve times in the head, arms, chest, stomach and legs. Still Durrant refused to yield, firing on the enemy destroyer with deadly accuracy.

Despite their best efforts, those aboard were overwhelmed by German fire. Every man aboard was wounded in the encounter and the ML damaged. There was no way they could now hope to break contact with the enemy so, reluctantly, the ML surrendered....

Eventually the men were put ashore at St. Nazaire. The severely wounded Sergeant Durrant was evacuated to the nearby civilian hospital but was to die of his wounds.

Meanwhile the dock was teaming with Germans and captured British. Only a matter of yards away Campbeltown and her explosive cargo sat silently at the dock gates....

It wasn't only the men of the MLs who were being brought into captivity. In St. Nazaire town, the German search effort was bearing fruits. Slowly but surely, small bands of commandos who were hiding to await the next night and with it their chance to break out into the countryside and possible freedom, were being rounded up....

Major Bill Copland, the second in command of the commando force, had been hiding in a cellar with a small group of his men. Copland knew that if the Germans found them there would be no possibility of escape. There were just too many wounded among his party and those still able to fight were only armed with a few pistols. Any attempt to force their way out of a compromise in daylight would see them quickly cut down. Given these facts, Major Copland decided that, if challenged, they would simply surrender.

A man who could speak fluent German and French was posted as a sentry at the entrance to the cellar. Major Copland had issued specific instructions that, if the enemy appeared, the man was to inform them that his comrades were hiding below and wished to give themselves up.

Even with the noise of vehicles and troops moving through the streets, Major Copland and his band of men still hoped that somehow they would be overlooked just long enough for darkness to fall....

Alas, while conducting a house to house sweep, one of the German search teams did find Major Copland's party. They were promptly taken prisoner and removed to a nearby restaurant where they met up with many other commandos and sailors who had fallen into enemy hands.

Despite being prisoners of war, the mood among the men was cheerful. They were all exhausted and most were wounded, but their spirit had in no way been dampened.

Although nobody said anything, each man was silently wondering if those damned charges aboard Campbeltown were ever going to go off....

Campbeltown's captain, Lieutenant-Commander Beattie, had been put ashore after a night spent floating in the Loire estuary. His rank insignia had marked him out for special attention and he was quickly brought for interrogation.

One of the Germans questioning Beattie knew he had some association with Campbeltown so remarked that, although the actions of the British had been gallant, any attempt to destroy the dry dock gates by simply ramming them with a destroyer was nothing but an exercise in futility. He assured Beattie that the damage done to the gates was easily repairable and that the ship would be refloated and removed within a matter of a week or two.

Just as the German officer was finishing his sentence an enormous explosion tore through the air. Such was its violence that the windows in the room into which Beattie had been taken were shattered.

Beattie knew exactly what the noise signified. For the Germans, confusion reigned momentarily as they attempted to find out what had happened…..

Over in the restaurant where the British POWs were being held, a cheer went up. The commandos and sailors knew that the Campbeltown had played out the final act of the drama….

There were over a hundred German troops aboard the Campbeltown when her charges went off. They were all killed in the blast, as were the 260 others who were milling about the vicinity. The sheer force of the explosion did exactly what Lieutenant Nigel Tibbits had designed it to do; tearing through the dry dock gates and wrecking them completely….

When they realised what had happened, it became apparent to the Germans that the British had not simply chosen to ram the dock gate in the hope of smashing through it. No, they had very carefully concealed a deadly payload of explosives which those who had searched Campbeltown failed to discover….

In the aftermath of the explosion the German hunt for evaders continued apace. They scoured both the town and the dock, looking in every place where someone could possibly hide....

Although the bulk of commandos had already been captured, there were still those who managed to slip the net. Although they were fragmented, operating singly or in small groups, each man knew that if they could remain at liberty until darkness they would have a chance of breaking through the enemy cordon then slipping unseen into the countryside beyond....

Captain Mickey Burn had hidden himself in the engine room of one of the boats moored in the Bassin de St-Nazaire. He had been joined by one of the commando privates during the night and together they had sought a suitable laying up place.

During the morning, Burn and his companion began to hear noises in close proximity to the boat. They knew that the Germans were searching the area. Sure enough the enemy boarded the boat and both men were discovered. They were marched through the streets at bayonet point to where the other POWs were being held. This particular incident was caught on camera and later appeared on German newsreels (the footage can also be viewed online should the reader wish to see it). Captain Burn can clearly be seen with his arms raised and holding his fingers in the Churchill 'V' (victory) sign. His hope was that the footage might somehow be seen by British intelligence and they would recognise his signal as confirmation that Operation Chariot had been a success.

Amazingly, the film was watched by British agents in occupied Europe who reported Captain Burn's signal to London....

Sergeant Major Haines was with a small group of men who were still hiding out in the town. Somehow they managed to stay one step ahead of the German search effort. In anticipation of the coming breakout attempt, the men realised they needed disguise themselves. An assortment of clothing was found in one of their hiding places and handed out between them.

When darkness came the group split into pairs and headed out of town. They were most careful to pick their way through areas which they thought safest. Just like the previous nights, they went through back gardens and over walls, sticking to the deepest shadows in order that they not be seen....

The man with Sergeant Major Haines was wearing an old civilian jacket over his uniform while Haines himself had donned a ladies overcoat. Once they had broken free into the countryside they planned to make their way to neutral Spain. The journey was in excess of 400 miles and both men knew that the Germans would be hunting them every step of the way.

Just as they were approaching the town limits, they walked straight into a German patrol and were promptly captured. For the Sergeant Major, the indignity of being caught wearing a woman's coat was almost too much to bear....

Five commandos, none above the rank of Corporal, managed to successfully evade the Germans, break out of the town then travel individually across country to Spain. Theirs was another example of human endurance and the commando ethos. With no food or support, and with the Germans actively searching, they finally arrived at the Spanish border, where they faced a trek through the Pyrenees in the face of strong border patrols.

All the men were later returned to Britain where they resumed their duties with the commandos....

For the majority of the 611 men who had taken part in the raid, their war was over. 169 men were killed while

215 were made prisoners of war. Most of the prisoners had sustained wounds to varying degrees of severity and after being tended to they were interrogated. The Germans wanted to know everything about the mission and how it had been planned. Where had the British gotten hold of the codes which allowed them to bluff their way past the shore defences protecting St Nazaire? How had they known where to find the pumping and winding houses at the Normandie dock? These and a myriad of other questions were put but met with the same stony silence. It quickly became apparent that all the captured sailors and commandos were prepared to reveal were their names, ranks and numbers....

Meanwhile, at the bottom of the old lock gates, the time delayed fuses in the two torpedoes fired by MTB 74 were quietly ticking away....

    The Germans knew the catastrophic extent of the damage wrought to the Normandie dock gates and the machinery which made the dry dock function, but they set about a clear up operation across the rest of the dockside.
    Slave labourers from the Organisation Todt were drafted in to rid the docks of debris. Although initial surveys confirmed that the Normandie dock was now unusable and would remain so for in indeterminate period of time, the orders from Berlin were to make sure the U-boats could operate and the wider installations put back into operation....

Out at sea, the three MLs headed by ML 160 managed to avoid further German attack as they made their way home. Disorientated and almost out of fuel, they happened upon a British convoy. They asked that the convoy escorts give them a navigational fix. Without knowing where the little boats had been, the Destroyers remarked about the 'bloody MLs always losing their way'. As it happened, ML 160 and the two other boats were just a few miles off Falmouth. With just enough fuel to reach land, they set off for home and safety….

When the battered trio of boats finally made port they were treated to an enthusiastic welcome. Sailors and dock workers lined the quaysides to wave and cheer them in.

News of the raid had already broken in the British media and everyone present knew that the MLs were sailing in straight from St. Nazaire. No doubts were left by the crowd as to their pride at the fantastic efforts of the Royal Navy and commando forces….

In London, Lord Mountbatten was in possession of the first batch of RAF aerial reconnaissance photographs of the Normandie dock and surrounding port area. The photographs didn't need the accompanying interpretation report, as it was obvious to see that the destruction was total.

After meeting with his Combined Operations staff, Mountbatten telephoned the Prime Minister and said "The Campbeltown's gone up sir!" Churchill was ecstatic. "This is great news." He replied. "This will keep Tirpitz out of the Atlantic for the rest of the war."

***

Two days after the attack, MTB 74s torpedoes exploded, taking their target with them. In the confusion the Germans thought the British were mounting another raid. They opened fire on anyone they saw; including each other. Several Todt workers were killed, along with sixteen French men, women and children.

When the Germans realised their mistake, they began to suspect sabotage. Innocent civilians were rounded up and a curfew placed on the town. Posters went up all over St.

Nazaire warning that further acts of subversion would result in random executions....

The Germans arranged military funerals for those who had paid the ultimate price. Amazingly, in an exceptional display of courage, many women from St. Nazaire turned up outside the building from where the dead British servicemen were to be taken to the graves. They were all in full mourning costume and followed the cortege to the burial site. Once at the cemetery the coffins were met by a party of captured commandos and sailors, whom the Germans had allowed to form a guard of honour. Upon seeing the British, the women broke through the German cordon to give food, money and best wishes to the POWs....

***

The Normandie dry dock remained out of action for the rest of the war. Churchill had been correct in his prediction that Tirpitz would never enter the Atlantic. With nowhere on the French coast to be refitted or repaired, Tirpitz spent the rest of her service confined to Norway. After taking part in actions against Russian bound British arctic convoys. She was eventually sunk by RAF Lancaster bombers of No's 9 and 617 (Dambusters) Squadrons in November 1944....

***

The Germans were astounded at the audacity of the mission and dumbfounded at how a Royal Navy flotilla had managed to pass right under the noses of the defenders on one of the most heavily guarded stretches of coast in occupied France.

Hitler was furious when he heard the news and demanded answers. He sacked the Chief of Staff to the Commander of OB West and his fury was felt all the way to the lowliest of troops who had been stationed in and around the St. Nazaire area....

Inquiries were held and many searching questions asked. The German military authorities had been unable to extract any information from the British commandos and seamen who were captured, so had to piece together a timeline of events from both their own and the British perspective as best they could....

What nagged Berlin most was the ongoing question of how the Royal Navy had come into possession of top secret Kriegsmarine pass codes. Had it not been for the attackers using these codes, the Germans agreed that they would have been stopped while still crossing the estuary. Their attempt to disguise HMS Campbeltown as a German destroyer, while passable in darkness, would itself have had little effect. It was the British ability to correctly answer the various challenges which allowed them to reach St. Nazaire....

Although they conducted exhaustive inquiries, Berlin never came close to finding the truth about the capture of the Kriegsmarine codebook and, more importantly, that their 'unbreakable' Enigma cypher system had been thoroughly compromised. They were so confident of its integrity of the Enigma system that they never for one minute suspected that this could be the case....

Hitler determined that nothing like this should happen again. Attention was focused on building fortified emplacements at all vulnerable points where it was suggested that the British might attempt a similar attack. The defences in and around St. Nazaire were strengthened and more coastal artillery batteries deployed to newly constructed concrete shelters....

The raid also served to remind the Germans just how vulnerable they were to attack from the sea along the whole of the western coast of occupied Europe. New impetus was given to the construction of the Atlantic coast defences and much money time and effort was expended in extending and fortifying the Atlantic Wall.

In a wider context, much needed resources – resources which were needed elsewhere – were diverted to the task of reinforcing the western coast defences. Troops, aircraft and tanks, which the Nazis otherwise would have deployed to Russia were also tied up indefinitely to defend against allied attack....

Aside from their collective fury that the raid had been allowed to happen, the Germans were also enraged because they mistakenly reached the conclusion that the British had meant to destroy the Normandie dry dock gate by means of a ramming attack. The subsequent explosion, they thought, was not intended to smash the gates but as a booby trap to kill or injure as many Germans as possible....

***

A total of 85 medals and 51 Mentioned in Dispatches were awarded to some of those who took part in Operation Chariot. One of the five Victoria Crosses awarded was presented posthumously to Sergeant Durrant. The Captain of the Kriegsmarine destroyer which had fought the short but furious engagement with

Durrant's ML as it attempted to escape back to England had been so astounded by the bravery of Durrant that it was he who had recommended the Sergeant for the VC. His report was passed via diplomatic channels in Spain and presented to the British. After reading what the German officer had to say, the British agreed that Sergeant Durrant should be awarded the highest gallantry decoration the country could bestow....

***

Citations for the Award of the Victoria Cross

LIEUTENANT-COLONEL AUGUSTUS CHARLES NEWMAN, VC. (Military Force Commander, Operation Chariot) On the night of 27th/28th March, 1942, Lieutenant-Colonel Newman was in command of the military force detailed to land on enemy occupied territory and destroy the dock installations of the German controlled naval base at St. Nazaire. This important base was known to be heavily defended and bomber support had to be abandoned owing to bad weather. The operation was therefore bound to be exceedingly hazardous, but Lieutenant-Colonel Newman, although empowered to call off the assault at any stage, was determined to carry to a successful conclusion the important task which had been assigned to him. Coolly and calmly he stood on the bridge of the leading craft as the small force steamed up the estuary of the River Loire, although the ships had been caught in the enemy searchlights and a murderous crossfire opened from both banks, causing heavy casualties.

Although Lieutenant-Colonel Newman need not have landed himself, he was one of the first ashore and, during the next five hours of bitter fighting, he personally entered several houses and shot up the occupants and supervised the operations in the town utterly regardless of his own safety, and he never wavered in his resolution to carry through the operation upon which so much depended. An enemy gun position on the roof of a U-boat pen had been causing heavy casualties to the landing craft and Lieutenant-Colonel Newman directed the fire of a mortar against this position to such effect that the gun was silenced. Still fully exposed, he then brought machinegun fire to bear on an armed trawler in the harbour, compelling it to withdraw and thus preventing many casualties in the main demolition area. Under the brilliant leadership of this officer the troops fought magnificently and held vastly superior enemy forces at bay, until the demolition parties had successfully completed their work of destruction. By this time, however, most of the landing craft had been sunk or set on fire and evacuation by sea was no longer possible.

Although the main objective had been achieved, Lieutenant-Colonel Newman nevertheless was now determined to try and fight his way out into open country and so give all the survivors a chance to escape. The only way out of the harbour area lay across a narrow iron bridge covered by enemy machine guns and although severely shaken by a German hand grenade, which had burst at his feet, Lieutenant Colonel Newman personally led the charge which stormed the position and under his inspiring leadership the small force fought its way to a point near the open country when, all ammunition expended, he and his men were finally overpowered by the enemy. The outstanding gallantry and devotion to duty of this fearless officer, his brilliant leadership and initiative, were largely responsible for the success of this perilous operation which resulted in heavy damage to the important naval base at St. Nazaire.

COMMANDER ROBERT EDWARD DUDLEY RYDER, VC, RN. (Naval Force Commander, Operation Chariot) For great gallantry in the attack on St. Nazaire. He commanded a force of small unprotected ships in an attack on a heavily defended port and led HMS Campbeltown in under intense fire at point blank range. Though the main object of the expedition had been accomplished in the beaching of Campbeltown, he remained on the spot conducting operations, evacuating men from Campbeltown and dealing with strong points and close range weapons while exposed to heavy fire for one hour and sixteen minutes, and did not withdraw till it was certain that his ship could be of no use in rescuing any of the Commando Troops who were still ashore. That his Motor Gun Boat, now full of dead and wounded, should have survived and should have been able to withdraw through an intense barrage of close range fire was almost a miracle.

LIEUTENANT- COMMANDER STEPHEN HALDEN BEATTIE, VC, RN. (In command: HMS Campbeltown) For great gallantry and determination in the attack on St. Nazaire in command of HMS Campbeltown. Under intense fire directed at the bridge from point blank range of about 100 yards, and in the face of the blinding glare of many searchlights, he steamed her into the dock gates and beached and scuttled her in the correct position. This Victoria Cross is awarded to Lieutenant-Commander Beattie in recognition not only of his own valour but also that of the unnamed officers and men of a very gallant ship's company, many of whom have not returned.

ABLE SEAMAN WILLIAM ALFRED 'BILL'

SAVAGE, VC. (Gunner, forward Oerlikon, MGB 314) For great gallantry, skill and devotion to duty as gunlayer of the Oerlikon in a motor gun boat in the St. Nazaire raid. Completely exposed and under heavy fire, he engaged positions ashore with cool and steady accuracy. On the way out of the harbour he kept up the same vigorous and accurate fire against the attacking ships, until he was killed at his gun. This Victoria Cross is awarded in recognition not only of the gallantry and devotion to duty of Able Seaman Savage, but also of the valour shown by many others, unnamed, in Motor Launches, Motor Gun Boats and Motor Torpedo Boats, who gallantly carried out their duty in entirely exposed positions against Enemy fire at very close range.

SERGEANT THOMAS FRANK DURRANT, VC. For great gallantry, skill and devotion to duty when in charge of a Lewis gun in HM Motor Launch 306 in the St. Nazaire raid on the 28th March, 1942. Motor Launch 306 came under heavy fire while proceeding up the River Loire towards the port. Sergeant Durrant, in his position aft of the bridge, where he had no cover or protection, engaged enemy gun positions and searchlights on shore. During this engagement he was severely wounded in the arm but refused to leave his gun. The Motor launch subsequently went down the river and was attacked by a German destroyer at 50 to 60 yards range, and often closer. In this action Sergeant Durrant continued to fire at the destroyer's bridge with the greatest of coolness and with complete disregard of the enemy's fire. The Motor Launch was illuminated by the enemy searchlight and Sergeant Durrant drew on himself the individual attention of the enemy guns, and was again wounded in many places. Despite these further wounds he stayed in his exposed position, still firing his gun, although after a time only able to support himself by holding onto the gun mounting. After a running fight, the Commander of the German destroyer called on the Motor Launch to surrender. Sergeant Durrant's answer was a further burst of fire at the destroyer's bridge. Although now very weak he went on firing, using drums of ammunition as fast as they could be replaced. A renewed attack by the enemy vessel eventually silenced the fire of the Motor Launch but Sergeant Durrant refused to give up until the destroyer came alongside, grappled the Motor Launch and took prisoner those who remained alive. Sergeant Durrant's gallant fight was commended by the German officers on boarding the Motor Launch. This very gallant Non Commissioned Officer later died of the many wounds received in action.

The following awards were also issued to members of the commandos and Royal Navy:

Four Distinguished Service Orders
Four Conspicuous Gallantry Medals
Five Distinguished Conduct Medals
Seventeen Distinguished Service Crosses
Eleven Military Crosses
Twenty Four Distinguished Service Medals
Fifteen Military Medals
Four Croix de Guerre
Fifty One Mentioned in Dispatches

The Flotilla

HMS Campbeltown: Destroyed by explosion at the Normandie dry dock.

MGB 314 (Headquarters boat): Damaged during the raid and withdrawal. Scuttled after rendezvousing with British destroyers.

MTB 74: Sunk during the withdrawal. Heavy loss of life.

ML 298: Sunk by enemy fire while off St. Nazaire port.

ML 306: Captured by the German destroyer 'The Jaguar' whilst attempting to return to England.

ML 307: Unable to land at the old mole. Returned to England

ML 341: Forced to retire before the mission Due to engine problems.

ML443: Unable to land at the old mole. Returned to England.

ML 446: Unable to land at the old mole. Damaged during the raid and withdrawal. Scuttled after rendezvousing with British destroyers.

ML 447: Sunk by enemy fire while attempting To land commandos at the old mole.

ML 457: Sunk by enemy fire after landing commandos at the old mole.

ML192: Hit by enemy fire off the old mole. Set ablaze and destroyed in the subsequent fire.

ML 262: Sunk by enemy fire during the withdrawal.

ML 267: Sunk by enemy fire off St Nazaire port.

ML 268.: Hit by enemy fire while astern of HMS Campbeltown
which caused her to blow up.

ML 156: Damaged during the raid and withdrawal. Scuttled after rendezvousing with British destroyers.

ML 160: After stopping to rescue those aboard ML 447 during
The withdrawal, she returned to England.

ML 177: Sunk by enemy fire during the withdrawal.

ML 270: Damaged during the raid and withdrawal. Scuttled after rendezvousing with British destroyers.

If you liked this book, then please consider leaving an
Amazon review. Thank you.

Please also keep watch for the next book in the
'They Who Dared' Series.

Printed in Great Britain
by Amazon